D0449388

The iPad
PocketGuide

Jeff **Carlson**

Ginormous knowledge, pocket-sized.

**Peachpit
Press**

The iPad Pocket Guide
Jeff Carlson

Peachpit Press
1249 Eighth Street
Berkeley, CA 94710
510/524-2178
510/524-2221 (fax)

Find us on the Web at: www.peachpit.com
To report errors, please send a note to errata@peachpit.com

Peachpit Press is a division of Pearson Education.

Editor: Clifford Colby
Copyeditor: Liane Thomas
Production editor: Cory Borman
Compositor: Jeff Carlson
Indexer: Ann Rogers
Cover design: Peachpit Press
Cover photography: Jeff Carlson
Interior design: Peachpit Press

ISBN-13:   978-0-321-71758-0
ISBN-10:   0-321-71758-9

9 8 7 6 5 4 3 2 1

Printed and bound in the United States of America

For Kimberly and Ellie

Acknowledgments

As I get to the end of a book project, I become more like a hermit in a cave, singularly focused on getting everything done on a tight time schedule. But books can't happen in isolation, and I was fortunate enough to have these wonderful people just outside the cave entrance, waiting with positive words and, on occasion, dessert.

This book exists because of the wonderful patience and encouragement from my wife Kim and my daughter Ellie.

My editor Cliff Colby shepherded the project from the beginning, while Cory Borman, Ann Rogers, and Liane Thomas put their amazing talents to work to create a high quality finished product.

Several people at Apple helped with answers to my questions, including Janette Barrios, Teresa Brewer, Keri Walker, and Khyati Shah.

My colleague Glenn Fleishman continues to be the best officemate, sounding board, and friend a guy could have.

My other officemates Kim Ricketts and Jenny Gialenes give me a reason to emerge from my home office cubby and experience the world.

Adam Engst and, especially, Tonya Engst, were supremely patient and helpful while I disappeared to finish this book.

Katie Lacey stepped up several times to take care of Ellie during crunch periods, and patiently let me ramble about esoteric iPad features without telling me to go away.

I'd like to say I had the idea first, but Scott Knaster inspired the caption on Figure 6.15.

About Jeff Carlson

Jeff Carlson gave up an opportunity to intern at a design firm during college because they really just wanted someone tall to play on their volleyball team. In the intervening years, he's been a designer and writer, authoring best-selling books on the Macintosh, Web design, video editing, and digital photography. He's currently a columnist for the *Seattle Times*, a senior editor of *TidBITS* (www.tidbits.com), and consumes almost too much coffee—almost. Find more information about him at jeffcarlson.com and neverenoughcoffee.com, and follow him on Twitter at @jeffcarlson.

Contents

Introduction

Given Apple's advertising budget and ubiquitous ads, plus an enormous amount of media attention, it's still difficult to determine just what an iPad *is*. Does it replace a laptop? Is it really just a "big iPod touch"? Is it a media player or a business machine? There are other tablet computers on the market, as well as "netbooks" that act like small laptops, and yet the iPad has captured people's imaginations and pocketbooks like few other devices I've seen. It took only 28 days for Apple to sell 1 million iPads, and that was just in the United States alone; those couldn't all be journalists and early adopters.

I've owned an iPad since the first day it was available, and I still have trouble explaining it to people. But I think I've figured out just what's so special about it.

The iPad is the first real *spontaneous* device. It's not as bulky as a laptop, and doesn't need to be anchored in one room of the house the way a desktop computer usually is. The iPad can be anywhere in the house, or with you on the bus or train, and is a godsend for anyone that frequently travels by air in cramped middle seats. You can pick it up and search for something, like an actor's name while watching TV, without having to relocate to "the computer" or trying to remember to look up the detail later. You can take the iPad into the kitchen and use an app such as Epicurious to find a menu and cook a meal.

At the same time, the iPad is not ultra compact the way a smartphone like the iPhone is. Although the iPad and iPhone share many of the same features—they're both based on the same underlying operating system, the iPhone OS—the iPad's larger screen does make a difference when interacting with software, viewing photos, and reading electronic books (even if your eyes don't see as well as they used to).

So what is the iPad? It's all of the things I mentioned, enhanced by the way you interact with it by touch. It's the first gadget in a long, long time that really makes a huge difference to use in person rather than just read about online. And it's also just the beginning: Apple thinks it's the future of computing, and I'm inclined to agree.

Conventions Used in this Book

The iPad is a computer, but it introduces a few new ways of interacting with software that differ from conventions used on computers running Microsoft Windows or Mac OS X. Here's how I refer to the following throughout the book.

Location of settings

Some applications (simply called *apps* in the iPad universe) include prefences within the apps, but Apple's preferred method is to make all settings available in the Settings app. From the iPad's Home screen, tap the icon labeled Settings (**Figure i.1**). Built-in apps and system functions appear at the top of the left pane, while third-party apps appear at the bottom. Tapping an app or service name reveals its settings in the right pane.

Figure i.1
The Settings app

Selected app —

Third-party apps —

Navigating settings

When I mention a preference in the Settings app, I do so with symbols to indicate the hierarchy of taps. So, when I write *Settings > Safari > AutoFill*, that translates to:

1. At the Home screen, tap the Settings app.

2. Tap the Safari button in the left-hand pane.

3. Tap the AutoFill button, part of Safari's preferences, in the right-hand pane.

Popovers

It's taken me a while to not think of breakfast pastry when I type this, but a "popover" (Apple's term) is a new interface element introduced on the iPad. A popover is a floating list of options that appears when you tap some buttons. In the iBooks app, for example, tapping the Fonts (_AA) button brings up a popover where you can change the text size and font of the main text (**Figure i.2**).

Figure i.2
A popover in iBooks

Popovers also often appear when you change the iPad's orientation in some apps. In the Mail app, for example, your Inbox appears in a pane at the left side of the screen when the iPad is in its landscape (wide) orientation. As soon as you rotate the iPad to portrait (tall), the Inbox sidebar becomes a popover.

Meet iPad

It's not often that something really new appears. Desktop and laptop computers are so commonplace, it's hard to believe that not too long ago you could go to the airport and see maybe one or two personal computers, total. The iPhone represented a new direction for Apple (and, it turns out, the cell phone industry), but it was still just a smartphone executed really well.

At first, the iPad doesn't seem particularly new. Companies—Apple included—have tried to create tablet computers for years and failed. So what makes the iPad different?

The iPad isn't the same old desktop software pressed into a laptop case that's missing a keyboard. It was designed from scratch to be a mobile tablet. And as you'll see when you use it and as you read this book, that's a profound difference. It's not a laptop replacement (although it wouldn't surprise me if it takes that role for some people), and it's not a limited handheld device, either. The iPad shares the same underlying operating system as the iPhone, so many aspects may be familiar if you already own an iPhone or iPod touch, but it doesn't rely on old computing crutches like using a mouse pointer or forcing the user to wrangle a sprawling file system.

Instead, the iPad is a big step forward based on an old, simple idea: anyone can take advantage of computing and digital media, without needing to be a computer expert—or even a "computer person." People shouldn't have to understand a hierarchical file system or virtual memory. This idea sounds simple, yet it's extremely difficult to do. And I think, even after years of making computers "for the rest of us," Apple is very close to doing it.

The iPad is the first step toward a new future. I'm not talking about robots and jet packs—though you might think I sound like I've spent too much time at a high altitude—but rather a dramatic break from what we expect computers to be. And that's a truly new idea.

Power On and Set Up the iPad

Out of the box, the iPad is an example of beautiful industrial design, but it can't do much. It needs to establish a connection with iTunes, where you set up basic information to get started. (If you've already done this stage, skip ahead to "iPad Essentials.")

1. Press and briefly hold the button at the top of the iPad until the Apple logo appears to power it on for the first time. Soon after, an image containing the iTunes logo and the sync cable appears.

2. On your computer, launch iTunes.

3. Connect the sync cable between the iPad and the computer.

4. In iTunes, register the iPad with Apple, or click the Register Later button.

5. Enter your Apple ID and password. This is the account you use to purchase media from the iTunes Store. If you don't already have an Apple ID, you can create one here.

6. If you subscribe to Apple's MobileMe service, enter your login (the @me.com or @mac.com email address) and password here. You can also try the service free for 30 days by clicking the Try It Free button.

Making the Case for MobileMe

Until recently, I've been a MobileMe (formerly .Mac) subscriber because I write about technology, not necessarily because I need yet another email account or iDisk online storage. However, now I recommend the service, for two reasons.

- MobileMe syncing allows you to keep your contacts, calendars, Web bookmarks, and other information up to date between the computer and the iPad (and iPhone, iPod touch, or other computers) without physically connecting to the computer. That's great for an always-connected device like the iPad Wi-Fi + 3G model or the iPhone.

- MobileMe includes the Find My iPad feature. If the iPad is lost or stolen, you can log in to me.com and view its location on a map; send a message or sound to it (if you think it might be nearby but you can't find it); or securely wipe the data remotely (if you think it may have been stolen).

7. Choose setup options:

- If you already sync to another iPhone or iPod touch, iTunes will (erroneously) report that "An iPad has been previously synced with this computer" and give you the option of copying the contents and settings from that device to the iPad. To use your existing data, choose Restore from the backup of [*the other device name*].

- If you'd prefer to set up the iPad from scratch, choose the Set up as new iPad option. Specify whether to automatically sync songs, photos, and applications.

- Click Done to finish setup, and then wait for the first sync to complete.

tip If you already have a lot of apps for your iPhone or iPod touch, iTunes may want to transfer them all to the iPad. Instead of deselecting unwanted apps one by one, do this: In the Apps tab in iTunes, Command-click (Mac) or Control-click (Windows) one app's checkbox to deselect them all. Then, go through the list and enable the apps you want to transfer.

note I own an iPhone 3GS, which goes with me everywhere. Because my iPad acts as an extension of all of my important data, I chose to use the data from my iPhone instead of configuring the iPad from scratch. If you take this route, you'll still need to do some cleanup work; I found that some universal iPad apps (ones which can run either on an iPhone or the iPad) did not transfer automatically, but otherwise the process was smooth.

iPad Essentials

After the iPad is set up, and each time you press the power button or Home button, a Slide to Unlock control appears. Drag your finger left to right along the slider to advance past the opening screen.

tip This may sound silly, but I've heard a lot of people complain that when they first turn on the iPad, it looks like the screen is already scratched! Don't worry, those streaks are stars in the long-exposure photo used as the default screen wallpaper. I talk about how to change the image later in this chapter.

Sleep and wake

Once powered on, the iPad rarely needs to be turned off. Instead, when you're finished using it, press the power button once (without holding it) to put it into a low-powered sleep mode.

note The iPad automatically goes to sleep after five minutes of inactivity to conserve battery power. You can change that amount in the Settings app by tapping General, then Auto-Lock, and tapping a time duration (1 to 5 minutes, or Never if you want to always put the iPad to sleep manually).

To wake the iPad, press the power button or the Home button and then use the Slide to Unlock control.

Power off

It's rare that I turn off the iPad completely —usually only when something seems to be wrong and I want to restart it, or if I know I won't be using it for an extended period of time (like *that's* realistic). To do so, press and hold the power button until the red Slide to Power Off control appears. Slide it to turn off the power.

tip To prevent just anyone from unlocking your iPad and accessing your data, specify a four-digit passcode that must be entered first. See Chapter 10 for more information.

Home screen

After you've unlocked the iPad, you're taken to the Home screen, which displays the software applications (or "apps") stored on the device (**Figure 1.1**). When your iPad holds more than 20 apps, a new Home screen is created; you can see how many screens are available by looking at the dots near the bottom of the screen. Swipe left or right to switch between each screen. The shelf at the bottom of the screen holds up to six apps that remain visible on every Home screen.

tip Yes, that's right. Although the shelf holds four apps initially (and four is the maximum number on the iPhone and iPod touch), you can add two more apps of your choosing.

Figure 1.1
Apps on the Home screen

Home button

Press the Home button in the bezel at any time to exit an app and go to the last Home screen you were viewing. If you press the button when you're already on a Home screen, you're taken to the first screen. Or, if you're currently viewing the first screen, pressing the button displays the Spotlight search page; see "Search Using Spotlight," later in this chapter.

Launch and run apps

Tap once on an app's icon to launch it. (That's it. No double-clicking, pressing Command-O, or hitting Return and wondering if Windows is actually opening the program.)

Unlike most desktop or laptop computers, the iPad runs one application at a time, which takes over the entire screen; it's not possible, for example, to have Mail on one side of the screen and Safari on the other. To switch to a different app, press the Home button and then tap the other app's icon from the Home screen.

note For more information about customizing the Home screen and working with apps, see Chapter 2.

Debunking the Multitasking Myth

When the iPad was announced, many people dismissed it (sight unseen) because it didn't support "multitasking." In the words of Inigo Montoya, "You keep using that word. I do not think it means what you think it means." The iPad does multitask, just not in the same way as a desktop computer. Some of the built-in apps can work in the background—for example, iPod can play music while you're using another app. However, the current version does not allow *third-party* apps to run in the background. So, multitasking is possible, but on a limited scale. Third-party multitasking will arrive soon, however: iPhone OS 4 is due for the iPad in Fall 2010.

Change screen orientation

One of the coolest features of the iPad is the accelerometer, a sensor inside that knows how the iPad is being held, including whether the screen is in a tall (portrait) or wide (landscape) orientation. Knowing the position is important, because the iPad's operating system adjusts to the orientation: Hold the Notes app in portrait position and the screen is filled with the yellow pad; rotate the display to the landscape position and a list of notes appears to the left of the pad (**Figure 1.2**).

Figure 1.2
Screen rotation

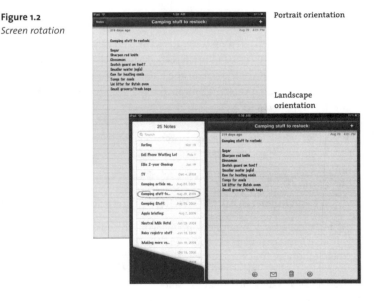

Portrait orientation

Landscape orientation

Simply turn the iPad to change its orientation. In fact, from the software's point of view, there is no "correct" orientation. No matter how you hold it, the screen contents rotate to be right-side up.

Screen orientation is just a parlor trick for the accelerometer, however. Because it calculates the iPad's position in three dimensions, it also knows at what angle you're holding the device and responds to that. Hundreds of games take advantage of the accelerometer, turning the entire iPad into the game controller to affect what's happening onscreen.

note Speaking of the screen, you'll notice that the iPad picks up fingerprints easily. Don't fret—the screen features an *oleophobic* surface, which means a swipe of your sleeve or a soft cloth will wipe the fingerprints away.

Lock screen rotation

There are times when you may not want the screen to adjust its orientation, like when you're reading while lying down. In this case, flick the Screen Rotation Lock button, located next to the volume adjustment buttons on the side, to freeze the current rotation. The accelerometer continues to react to other motion.

Adjust screen brightness

Normally, the iPad's ambient-light sensor adjusts the screen brightness automatically according to its surroundings. If you'd like to dim the light or punch it up manually, go to Settings > Brightness & Wallpaper and drag the slider left (darker) or right (brighter). To always adjust manually, turn off the Auto-Brightness switch.

tip Dimming the brightness is one of the best tactics for conserving battery life, especially because of the iPad's expansive screen.

Battery

The iPad includes a non-removable lithium-polymer battery that provides, according to Apple, up to 10 hours of use on a single charge.

(In fact, Apple claims 10 hours of video playback, surfing the Web using Wi-Fi, or listening to music are possible.)

Actual battery life depends on how you use the iPad, of course—playing a video game that makes extensive use of 3D graphics is more demanding on the processor and will eat up power faster than reading a book in iBooks. As the battery nears depletion, warning messages appear when 20 percent and 10 percent of the power remains. After that, the iPad becomes unresponsive and needs to be charged to function again.

Recharging the iPad

The only accessories that come with the iPad are a sync cable and a power adapter. Plug the cable into the iPad and the adapter to replenish the battery's charge (a process that takes about four hours if the battery is nearly spent).

You can also plug the sync cable into your computer to sync and recharge, but there's a catch: your computer's USB port may not have the oomph to do it. If that's the case, you'll see "Not Charging" in the power indicator at the upper-right corner of the screen.

The specifications for running power over USB call for at least 5V (Volts), but the iPad requires more than that. Some computers, such as recent Apple laptops and desktops, can optionally provide as much as 12V when a device that requires it is connected. In that case, the iPad will charge, but slower than when connected to the power adpater.

The upside is that when connected to a USB port, the battery doesn't seem to deplete; it just doesn't provide additional charge. If you find yourself in that situation, be sure to keep the iPad's power adapter nearby.

You can take steps to make the most of the battery's charge. No need to be slavish about these, but you'll definitely want to implement them when you get a low battery notice:

- Turn down the screen brightness.

- Turn off Wi-Fi if you're not within range of a wireless network.

- Turn off Bluetooth if you're not using it.

- Disable Push notifications (see Chapter 2).

- Disable 3G networking (if you own the 3G model) if you're not accessing data online (discussed later in this chapter).

tip To help prolong the battery's lifespan, once a month charge the iPad to 100 percent and don't charge it again until the battery reaches zero. Then, charge it back to 100 percent. Apple offers more information at www.apple.com/batteries/ipad.html.

What if the battery dies?

Batteries lose capacity over time, but sometimes a battery won't hold a charge for nearly as long as it once did. If the iPad is still under warranty (one year, or two years if you also purchased AppleCare for it), contact Apple and ask for a replacement. If an Apple retail store is nearby, an Apple Genius will be able to diagnose whether the battery is faulty.

If you're out of warranty and the iPad "requires service due to the battery's diminished ability to hold an electrical charge," in Apple's words, then you can take advantage of Apple's battery replacement service. For $99, Apple will replace the entire iPad (so be sure you've synchronized it before sending it off). See www.apple.com/support/ipad/service/battery/ for more information.

Multi-Touch Gestures

You'll notice that when you opened the iPad's box, no stylus fell out. Until recently, most tablet computers and handhelds required that you use a plastic pencil to do anything. The iPad, instead, is designed for your fingers. You interact with the software on the screen by touching, tapping, swiping, and performing other Multi-Touch gestures. Many controls are intuitive: tap the Edit button in Contacts, for example, to edit a person's information. Other motions may not be obvious at first, but quickly become natural.

Tap

The most obvious action is to point at an area of the screen, like a button or other control, and lightly tap with one finger. Sometimes, you'll want to double-tap the screen, such as when you want to zoom in on a section of a Web page in Safari.

 When you encounter an On/Off switch, you can slide the switch if you want, or simply tap it to change its state.

Touch and hold

Instead of quickly tapping and lifting your finger from the screen, there are times when you want to touch the screen and maintain contact to elicit an action (for example, see "Work with Text," ahead).

Drag

Touch and hold a point on the screen, then move your finger across the glass. Drag a Web page in Safari from bottom to top to scroll as you read.

Flick and swipe

A flick (yes, that's Apple's official name for it) is like a drag, but faster. On a Web page as above, touch the screen and flick your finger to "throw" the page in any direction. The software simulates the physics of the motion and slows the scrolling page until it comes to a stop, based on the velocity of the flick.

A swipe is similar to a flick, but you drag something (usually horizontally) a bit slower. You swipe a photo from right to left to advance to the next picture, for instance.

Pinch

When you want to zoom in or out on an item, such as a map, a photo, or a Web page, touch two fingers to the screen and pinch them together (to zoom out) or spread them apart (to zoom in).

Rotate

Press two fingers to the screen and rotate them in a circle to rotate something such as a photo in the Photos app.

Shake

Yes, that's right, give the iPad a good shake. The accelerometer recognizes the motion as an intentional vibration, and software that's been written to handle the gesture can act on it. For example, when you're typing in the Notes app and make a mistake, shake the iPad to bring up a dialog that gives you the option to undo the last action. I've found that shaking front to back, not side-to-side, seems to be more responsive.

note The iPad's screen responds to the electricity in your fingers, not pressure. Pressing harder on the display won't improve its response.

Use Two Hands

The iPad's entire screen is filled with sensors, so take advantage of the large display area and use both hands. One obvious application is the keyboard that appears when you're entering text; since it's nearly full size, you can type as you would on a physical keyboard.

For another example, look to Apple's Keynote app: touch and hold a slide with the finger of one hand, and then use your other hand to tap other slides to select them all in a group. Numerous games and other apps also accept two-handed input.

Work with Text

It's one thing to view photos and movies, but how do you enter and edit text? Whether you're typing a Web address, adding an event to your calendar, or composing a letter, you need to know how to put letters to screen. You'll encounter the following basic operations throughout the iPad environment.

Type text

Whenever you tap on an editable text area, the iPad's software keyboard slides up from the bottom of the screen (**Figure 1.3**). Type on it as you would a regular keyboard, keeping a few things in mind:

- The screen can't accommodate a full-sized keyboard, so some characters appear where you may not expect them. For example, you type an exclamation point (!) by holding the Shift (⇧) key and tapping the comma (,) key. Number keys are accessed by tapping the ".?123" key, and symbols such as the equals-sign (=) are available after next tapping the "#+=" key.

- The keyboard varies depending on the context of the text field. When you're in the Address field in Safari, you'll see a ".com" key—a shortcut for the often-typed end to a Web address—and the Return key reads "Go". At other times, you may not see letters at all, such as when a number keypad and options for different functions appear when you edit values in Numbers.

Figure 1.3
The onscreen keyboard

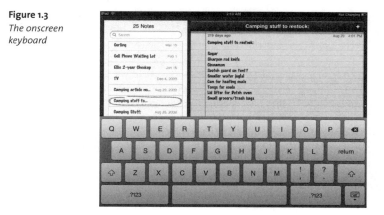

tip   To quickly enter other domain name suffixes like .net or .org, touch and hold the ".com" key. A pop-up menu presents other options for you to tap to add to the text. The same is true for typing accented characters.

- To hide the keyboard without exiting the text field, tap the (⌨) key.

- You can end a sentence with a period by simply tapping two spaces after a word. This shortcut came about on the iPhone, where the period key doesn't appear on the first screen of keys. If you'd rather turn off this feature, go to Settings > General > Keyboard and disable the "." Shortcut option.

tip Want to know the most useful iPad keyboard tip? To type an apostrophe, which isn't on the main screen, touch the comma (,) key and slide your finger up to insert the apostrophe character.

- By default, the Caps Lock feature is disabled (nobody likes it when PEOPLE SHOUT, after all), but if you often type acronyms or otherwise want the option, go to Settings > General > Keyboard and turn on the Enable Caps Lock option. When typing, quickly double-tap the Shift key to enter Caps Lock mode; the face of the key is highlighted (versus just the up-arrow icon when normal Shift is active).

note If you look closely at the software keyboard, you'll see faux raised bumps on the F and J keys, which on a physical keyboard help touch-typists determine their finger position without looking at the keys. There's no raised portion of glass on the screen, of course, but it's a subtle visual clue, meant to make you feel more at home typing on the smooth surface. All sorts of little "real-world" touches like this one are scattered throughout the iPad interface.

Auto-Correction

This extremely helpful feature debuted on the iPhone, where the smaller screen size makes it more challenging to hit the right keys as you're typing. As you type, the iPad analyzes your letters to look for patterns and offers suggestions in a little pop-up box (**Figure 1.4**). To accept the suggestion, type a space or punctuation. To ignore it, either tap the X on the pop-up or continue typing letters. (Also see "Cut, Copy, Paste, and Replace" two pages ahead.)

Go to Settings > General > Keyboard if the feature is getting in your way. While there, you can also disable Auto-Capitalization, which automatically enables the Shift key after you've applied punctuation.

Figure 1.4
Text auto-correction

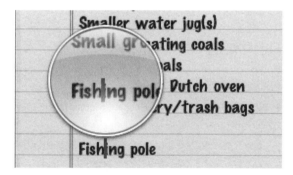

Select text

On a computer, selecting text is easy: you position your mouse pointer, then click and drag to select the text you want. The iPad has no mouse pointer, so the process of selecting text is slightly different.

1. Within any range of text (not just in text-entry fields), touch and hold where you want to start selecting. A magnified view of the area appears above your finger (**Figure 1.5**).

Figure 1.5
Select text with magnification.

2. Position the insertion point and release your finger. As you'll see in a moment, you don't need to put the insertion point at the exact start of your selection.

3. In the pop-up that appears, choose Select to highlight the closest word; or, tap Select All to highlight a full sentence.

4. Drag the handles to the left and right of the initial selection to define the full area you wish to select. If you drag beyond a paragraph, the selection area broadens to include blocks of text instead of letter-by-letter selections.

tip If you're in an editable text area (versus a read-only area like a Web page), double-tap a word to select it. Or, tap four times quickly to select an entire sentence. Or, here's a quick tip that doesn't apply just to editable areas: double-tap a word, but hold the second tap to make a selection, and then drag to expand it without lifting your finger.

note Selecting text occasionally works differently depending on which app you're using. In Safari, for example, touching and holding on text on a Web page selects whichever word is under your finger; drag to select any word, lift your finger, and then expand the selection.

Cut, Copy, Paste, and Replace

When you make a selection, a set of options appears above the text (**Figure 1.6**).

- **Cut:** The selection is copied to memory and then removed from the content you're editing.

- **Copy:** The selected content is just copied to memory.

- **Paste:** If you've previously cut or copied some text, the Paste option appears. Tap Paste to add the content stored in memory; if a selection is made, the pasted content overwrites the selection.

- **Replace:** Does a word look misspelled? Select it and tap the Replace button. If the iPad comes up with a different spelling (or a similar

word), it appears in a pop-up—tap the suggestion to replace the
selected word.

tip Selecting, copying, and pasting aren't reserved solely for text. In
Safari, for example, you can select a range of text that also includes an
image, copy it, and then open Mail and paste the content into an outgoing
message.

Figure 1.6
Selection options

After choosing
the Replace option

Sync with a Computer

Although by itself the iPad may do everything you need, it still must
connect to a Mac or Windows PC to transfer your media, manage your
personal information, back up its data, and download important software updates. Don't worry, this doesn't mean you're forever shackled by
that 30-pin USB cable—just that the iPad needs to check in occasionally.

The iPad's home base is iTunes, Apple's media hub software. If you don't
have the latest version, go to www.apple.com/itunes/ to download and
install it.

When you connect the iPad using the USB cable, the iPad appears in the iTunes sidebar. Select it to view information and options for synchronizing your data (**Figure 1.7**).

Figure 1.7
The iPad in iTunes

iPad in sidebar

Here's what gets transferred when you connect the iPad:

- Any new or changed data, which is added to the backup of the iPad on your computer

- Personal information such as calendars and contacts (unless you're syncing over the air; see Chapter 9)

- New and updated apps (those downloaded on the iPad and in iTunes)

- Music, movies, and TV shows

- Podcasts

- iTunes U (university courses available via iTunes)

- Photos

- Files used by iPad apps

If This Is Your First Sync

The first time you connect the iPad to your computer, iTunes performs an initial sync and gives you the option to transfer your entire music and video library (space permitting). If there isn't enough room, you can choose which items are copied over. See Chapter 7.

The iPad runs the same operating system as the iPhone and iPod touch, so if you already own one of these devices, any apps you've purchased will automatically be transferred to the iPad during the first sync.

However, that means *all* apps you own including ones that are not currently installed on your iPhone or iPod touch. If you've removed apps from the device, they still reside in iTunes. Depending on the number of apps, this situation may mean just a few more minutes during the initial sync. If you've gone app-crazy, you may want to cancel the sync (click the cancel button (⊗) in the iTunes status display) and then manually choose which apps are transferred within the Applications tab. (You don't have to click every box individually. To deselect all apps, Command-click on the Mac or Control-click under Windows.) See "Find and Install Apps" in Chapter 2 for more details.

note You'll be surprised at just how infrequently you may need to sync the iPad. Using MobileMe, for example, you can wirelessly sync your calendars and contacts. Application updates are also available using the included App Store app (see Chapter 2).

Disconnect the iPad

When you want to take the iPad somewhere, simply disconnect the sync cable. Unlike other USB devices, it doesn't need to be ejected first.

Special sync options

Synchronization mostly concerns transferring your media and related files. These options, found on the Summary screen, refine how iTunes handles the sync.

- **Automatically sync this iPad when connected:** Enable this option to initiate a sync as soon as you plug in the iPad. If it's disabled, you must start each sync by selecting the iPad in iTunes and clicking the Sync button.

- **Sync only checked songs and videos:** In iTunes, you can disable a song's checkbox to prevent it from playing (such as when you like every song on an album except one). If this option is unchecked, all songs and movies are copied to the iPad, taking up memory.

- **Prefer standard definition videos:** Although the iPad can play Apple's HD videos, they take up much more memory. Mark this option to transfer standard definition versions of movies to conserve storage.

- **Manually manage music and videos:** Wield more control over what gets transferred to the iPad. When this option is enabled, you can drag songs and videos from your iTunes library to the iPad name in the sidebar. If you decide to turn off this feature later, however, your music and videos are erased and replaced according to the options you set up in each media tab.

- **Convert higher bitrate songs to 128 kbps AAC:** Enabling this option can significantly reduce the amount of space your music collection occupies by making lower (but still decent) quality versions of songs.

- **Encrypt iPad backup:** Your personal data on the iPad is encrypted—scrambled so that if the iPad is lost or stolen, its contents can't be read. The backup stored on your computer's hard disk, however, is not encrypted. To make it inaccessible to prying eyes, activate this option.

A dialog appears asking you to define a password and verify it. See Chapter 10 for more information about iPad security.

- **Configure Universal Access:** Click this button to enable options that make the iPad more usable for people with impaired vision or hearing. These controls mirror those found in Settings > General >Accessibility.

tip What if you want to connect the iPad to your computer but don't want to sync? You can't change the automatic sync preference without the iPad connected. Instead, press and hold Command-Option (Mac) or Shift-Control (Windows) when you connect the iPad, and hold them until the iPad appears in the sidebar. It won't sync.

Update the system software

When Apple releases updates to the iPhone OS, which powers the iPad, iTunes informs you with an alert. You can also click the Check for Update button on the Summary screen to query manually. If an update is available, you're given the option of downloading and installing it.

tip If you say yes to the update, you get to choose between downloading and installing it right away, or just downloading the software for later. The second option is good if you want to take advantage of a robust Internet connection (for example, you're at the office or in a coffee shop with your laptop) but plan to update the iPad at another time (such as when you get home).

iTunes backs up the contents of the device before applying the update, so your data is safe. The update process can take a while, so make sure you have an available block of time (say, at least 30 minutes to be safe) available before applying the update.

The iPad needs to restart during the process. When it's finished, the new software revision appears at the top of the Summary screen.

Connect to the Internet Using Wi-Fi

Every iPad supports Wi-Fi wireless networking, enabling you to connect to the Internet using nearby access points; you may have a Wi-Fi network set up in your house or office, or you might go to a nearby "hotspot," usually a coffee shop or restaurant. A Wi-Fi network usually covers the space of a house or small building. Compare that to 3G cellular wireless (more on that shortly), which is designed to offer miles of coverage.

Once the iPad is connected to a Wi-Fi network, you can browse the Web, send and receive email, view maps, and perform other tasks that require an Internet connection. Wi-Fi also lets you interact with other devices and computers sharing the network connection; for example, you can play a game against another iPad owner or control music playback of a computer running iTunes.

Choose a Wi-Fi access point

When the iPad requires an Internet connection, such as accessing email or a Web page, it checks to see if there's an active Wi-Fi network within range. A dialog appears with a list of nearby networks (**Figure 1.8**). Tap the name of a network you want to join, type its password if required, and then tap the Join button on the keyboard.

Figure 1.8
Available Wi-Fi networks

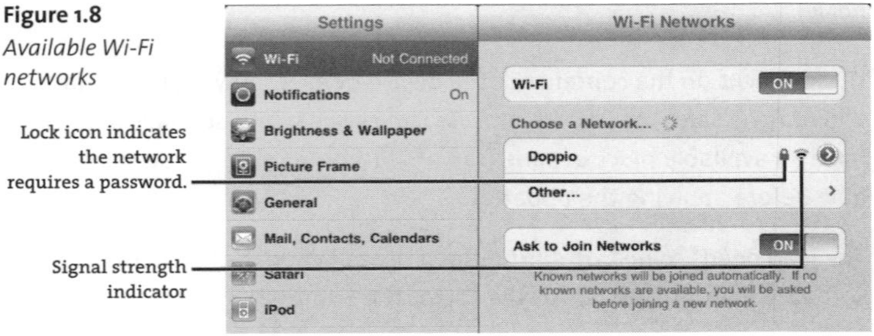

Lock icon indicates the network requires a password.

Signal strength indicator

Settings	Wi-Fi Networks
Wi-Fi — Not Connected	Wi-Fi — ON
Notifications — On	Choose a Network...
Brightness & Wallpaper	Doppio
Picture Frame	Other...
General	
Mail, Contacts, Calendars	Ask to Join Networks — ON
Safari	Known networks will be joined automatically. If no known networks are available, you will be asked before joining a new network.
iPod	

note Many public Wi-Fi hotspots don't require a password to join the network, but do need you to log in using a Web form once you're connected. After you get onto the network, go to Safari and enter any valid **Web** address. A login page should appear if you need to sign in (or pay) for access.

tip If you'd rather not be interrupted by a pop-up list of networks, go to Settings > Wi-Fi and then turn off the Ask to Join Networks option.

tip Exercise good judgment when joining open, unprotected Wi-Fi networks. It's possible (and easy, for those who are savvy) to intercept the data passing between the iPad and the base station running the network. A nefarious network owner—or even someone at the next table in a coffee shop—could collect the data stream and mine it for things like passwords and credit card numbers. Unless you can vouch for the network owner, avoid paying bills or making purchases on public networks. See Chapter 10 for more information.

Connect to a Wi-Fi network manually

The iPad is helpful in displaying and connecting available Wi-Fi networks, but there are times when you will want to link up with one manually—if you accidentally connected to the wrong network, or the owner has hidden the network name for security, for instance. Here's how to connect using the Settings app.

1. Tap Settings > Wi-Fi.

2. From the list that appears under Choose a Network, tap a network name.

3. If a password is required, type it into the Password field and then tap the Join button.

The network name gains a checkbox and a Wi-Fi signal strength icon appears in the upper-left corner of the screen.

To connect to a network that isn't broadcasting its name, or if the iPad isn't listing the one you expect, do the following:

1. In the Wi-Fi screen, tap the Other button.

2. Type the network name in the Name field.

3. Tap the Security button and specify which type of encryption the network is using. If you don't know, try WPA2 first, followed by WEP (which is older and no longer secure, but still widely used).

4. Enter the network's password in the Password field that appears.

5. Tap Join to establish a connection.

Use a Cellular Data Network with a Wi-Fi iPad

Instead of purchasing an iPad with Wi-Fi and 3G, some people are employing a different technique to provide ubiquitous Internet access.

The Novatel Wireless MiFi (www.novatelwireless.com) and Sprint's Overdrive (www.sprint.com/overdrive) are portable Wi-Fi hotspots that connect to a cellular data network. They're both pocket-sized and offer the same type of always-on connection that the iPad 3G provides. However, they're not bound to one carrier, and they can let more than one device connect at a time.

(It would be great if the iPad could act as a Wi-Fi base station and share its connection with a laptop, but that's not the case.)

The monthly service costs more than the iPad 3G's setup (as of late April 2010, that is), but you're not tied to Apple's preferred carrier. If you need to connect several devices over Wi-Fi (like the iPad, an iPhone, and a laptop), or you can't get good reception using your cellular provider, something like the MiFi may be perfect.

> **tip** The iPad remembers Wi-Fi network names and settings, so the next time you're within range of a network you've previously joined, a connection is automatically made.

Disconnect from a Wi-Fi network

If you accidentally join the wrong network, it's easy to sever the connection. In Settings > Wi-Fi, tap the detail button (⊙) and then tap Forget this Network.

Turn off Wi-Fi

Go to Settings > Wi-Fi and set the Wi-Fi switch to Off. You may want to do this when conserving battery power or if you're in an area where you know a Wi-Fi network isn't available.

Connect to the Internet Using 3G

For people who tend to travel more, or need more frequent access to the Internet than is afforded by Wi-Fi hotspots, Apple offers an iPad model with 3G cellular data access built in, the same network used by modern cell phones. With 3G enabled, your iPad likely has Internet access nearly everywhere.

However, 3G is more expensive: the 3G iPad model costs $130 more than the Wi-Fi–only model in the United States and requires an additional fee to access the network. The good news is that Apple negotiated a great deal with AT&T to provide 3G access. (As I write this, 3G details have been announced only for the U.S. market. By the time you read this, Apple should have announced international pricing; see www.apple.com/ipad/3g/.)

note The iPad can hop onto a 3G cellular network, but it can't place or receive calls like an iPhone. The 3G access is strictly for data. (But you can still place calls using a Voice-over-IP service such as Skype.)

Here's how it works: For $14.99, you can transfer—both downloads and uploads—250 megabytes (MB) of data within a 30-day period. For $29.99, you get unlimited data transfer during the same period. The "great" part is that, unlike the iPhone, there's no contract that locks you in for a minimum length of time. Activate the plan when you need it (if you expect to travel a lot next month, for instance), and cancel when you're done. If you bump against the 250 MB limit of the first plan, you can jump to the unlimited plan or wait until the 30-day cycle begins again.

And you do it all from the iPad directly.

tip The 3G iPad boasts two other differences over the Wi-Fi model. It includes a GPS chip for identifying the iPad's position in Maps and other apps; the Wi-Fi model uses a method based on wireless access points to determine its location. (See Chapter 8 for more information.) Also, when a 3G plan is active, you get free Wi-Fi access at AT&T-operated Wi-Fi hotspots, such as those in Starbucks, McDonalds, and many airports.

Activate 3G service

To enable cellular service, do the following:

1. Go to Settings > Cellular Data and make sure the Cellular Data option is set to On (**Figure 1.9**).

2. Tap the View Account button.

3. Enter your user information.

4. Enter login information. This is a new account for the iPad, not an existing account with your provider. (So even if you have an iPhone account, the iPad is separate.) Type an email address and a new password.

Figure 1.9
Cellular Data preferences

5. Tap a plan to choose it (**Figure 1.10**).

Figure 1.10
Signing up for 3G service

6. Enter your credit card and billing information and tap Next.

7. Read the terms of service and tap Agree.

8. Review the payment summary and tap Done.

After a few minutes, a dialog appears informing you that your data plan has been successfully activated.

Once 3G service is activated, you can access the Internet anywhere you have cellular reception.

 If you know you're going to spend a lot of time using Wi-Fi, disable the 3G radio temporarily to conserve battery life.

Measure your 3G data usage

So, just how far will you get with 250 MB of data? As you might expect, that depends on your use. Go to Settings > General > Usage. The Cellular Network Data section tells you how much data you've used, how much remains (if it's the 250 MB plan), and how many days are left in the billing period.

note In an area where both Wi-Fi and 3G work, Wi-Fi supercedes the cellular network. Using the iPad at a Wi-Fi hotspot, for example, doesn't count toward the data limit even if 3G service is active.

Add or cancel 3G service

As you approach the end of the allotted bandwidth on the 250 MB plan, the iPad displays warnings when you reach 20 percent of data left, then 10 percent, and then zero. At any point, if you want to add bandwidth, tap the Now button to bring up the Cellular Data Plan window. You can also get there at any time by going to Settings > Cellular Data and tapping Add Data or Change Plan. Choose to add another 250 MB for an additional $14.99; switch to the Unlimited plan for $29.99; or cancel the plan (**Figure 1.11**).

Figure 1.11
Change 3G plan options

note International roaming data rates can be substantially higher than what your domestic carrier offers, so if you know you'll be traveling out of the country, tap the Add International Plan button and set up a plan (Figure 1.12)

Figure 1.12
*International
3G data plans*

tip The SIM card included with the iPad 3G stores your name and account information. You can remove it from the iPad and put it into another device that accepts a Micro SIM card and still use your account. It ships with a PIN code that's set by the network provider. To lock the SIM card for added security, tap the SIM PIN button in the Cellular Data settings, switch SIM PIN to On, and enter 1111 (the default for AT&T in the U.S.). To set a new code, tap Change PIN and follow the instructions. (If you enter the wrong passcode three times, the SIM is shut down, and you need to contact the cellular provider to re-activate it. See http://support.apple.com/kb/HT4113 for more information.)

Connect to Bluetooth Devices

The iPad includes just two ports for connecting cables: the headphone port at the top and the dock port at the bottom. The rest of the iPad's communication happens wirelessly via Wi-Fi, 3G, or a third option: Bluetooth. Thanks to this short-range wireless technology, you can listen to music using Bluetooth headphones or speakers; you can also

type using any Bluetooth keyboard instead of the onscreen keyboard or
Apple's optional keyboard dock accessory.

> **note** When shopping for Bluetooth audio products, look for ones that
> support A2DP (Advanced Audio Distribution Profile).

Pair the iPad and the device

To communicate with the iPad, a Bluetooth device must be *paired* with it
to ensure that each device is recognized and won't get confused by other
Bluetooth connections nearby. You need to pair the devices only once,
after which the iPad identifies and communicates with the keyboard or
audio product automatically when it's within range. Follow these steps:

1. Open the Settings app and tap the General category.

2. Tap the Bluetooth option.

3. Ensure that Bluetooth is on; if not, slide the Bluetooth switch to On.

4. Power on the Bluetooth device you want to pair and put it into its
   pairing mode; you may need to press and hold a button on the device
   to switch modes. It will appear in the list of Devices (**Figure 1.13**).

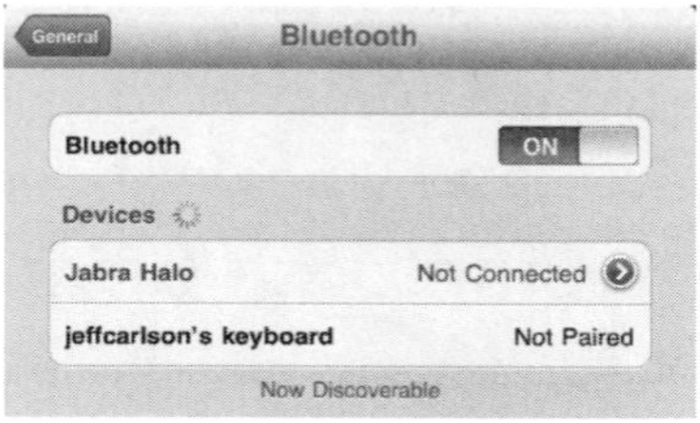

Figure 1.13
*Paired and
unpaired devices*

5. If the iPad displays a dialog for pairing, skip to the next step.
   Otherwise, tap the name of the unpaired device.

6. Enter the device's PIN number.

For headsets this is usually "0000" (four zeros) but check the device's instructions if that doesn't work.

For keyboards, the PIN is a series of numbers that appears on the iPad screen and the Return or Enter key (**Figure 1.14**).

Figure 1.14
Pairing the Apple Wireless Keyboard

"jeffcarlson's keyboard" would like to pair with your iPad.

Enter the passkey "956974" on "jeffcarlson's keyboard", followed by the return or enter key.

Cancel

7. Tap the Connect button. If successful, the device appears as Connected on the Bluetooth screen.

> **tip** The iPad can be paired with more than one device at the same time. For example, you can listen to music through a wireless Bluetooth headset while typing on a Bluetooth keyboard.

> **tip** When using a Bluetooth keyboard, the iPad's onscreen keyboard won't appear. This makes sense, except when you're close enough to be in range of the keyboard but not intending to use it. You may need to go into Settings and disable Bluetooth in that case (or turn off the keyboard's power, but is it really worth getting off the couch to do that?).

> **tip** I bought the Apple Wireless Keyboard to use with my iPad, but you can use nearly any Bluetooth keyboard. When you want to turn off the Apple model without disabling Bluetooth on the iPad, press and hold the power button for a few seconds until you see the status light disappear.

Forget the Bluetooth device

To remove a device from the list, tap the detail button (●) and then tap the Forget this Device button.

Search Using Spotlight

Even the smallest-capacity iPad model stores a lot of information. To locate something quickly, go to the Home screen and swipe to the right. (If you're in any Home screen, you can also press the home button twice; one press takes you to the first Home screen, and the second opens the Spotlight screen. Don't be too quick about the two button presses, though: an option in the Settings app allows a *double-press* to perform an action, like launching a specific app.)

Type some text into the Search field to bring up results, sorted by apps (**Figure 1.15**). Tap the one you want to jump to it.

Figure 1.15
*Spotlight
search results*

App

iPod music

To quickly erase a term and start over, tap the X icon to the right of the Search field.

tip Spotlight also matches app names when you search, so if you have dozens of apps and don't want to navigate to the screen containing the one you want, simply perform a Spotlight search to locate and launch it.

2

Getting and Using Apps

The iPad is sleek and shiny, a fantastic example of industrial design that packs a host of cutting-edge technologies into a thin, responsive tablet. Aside from holding it in your hand, however, your time spent using the iPad will be focused almost entirely on its software.

The core apps that ship with the iPad are useful, but those are just the beginning. More than 150,000 (at this writing) programs are available from the App Store—so many that Apple's marketing tagline, "There's an app for that," has become part of current popular culture.

With a few taps (and often just a few dollars), you can locate, purchase, and download apps that do nearly anything you can think of. In this chapter, I tell you how to find and install apps, and also how you can share them with friends.

Find and Install Apps

Quick, jump in the car, let's go app shopping!

Or don't. In the case of most software, buying new programs means going to a store in the mall, or buying a box from an online retailer, or even downloading it from the developer directly. But that's not the case with iPad apps.

The only outlet to get apps is Apple's App Store, available on the iPad itself or from within iTunes. Pricing varies among apps, naturally, but most cost less than $15—in many cases, far less, with many apps available for free.

note The App Store does not offer demo or shareware versions of apps, so it's difficult to evaluate an app before purchasing it. It's not impossible, though: Many vendors offer free "light" versions of their apps, which are limited in scope but give you a sense of what the paid version can do. Other apps may cost as little as $0.99 and offer just a handful of features, with the option to unlock others if you pony up some more cash.

The App Store on the iPad

Tap the App Store icon on the Home screen to launch the App Store. Since it's a storefront, you'll see many new and featured titles, including apps that are designed specifically for the iPad (**Figure 2.1**).

The screen is broken up into several areas. The In the Spotlight section at top provides a Cover Flow view of featured apps. Flick left and right to bring the apps to the front of the view and tap one that interests you. The boxed New and Noteworthy section reveals more showcase items.

note In an odd interface discrepancy, you must tap the arrow buttons at the edges of the boxed areas to view more items, instead of swiping left or right as in the Spotlight area at the top of the page.

Figure 2.1
*The App Store
on the iPad*

Swipe left or right to
view spotlight apps.

Tap arrows to
view more apps
in boxed areas.

The first three buttons at the bottom of the screen let you view featured apps, consult lists of the most popular paid and free apps in Top Charts, or browse by category. (See "Update Apps," later in this chapter, for more about the Updates button.) If you already know what you're looking for, enter its name into the Search field in the upper-right corner of the screen.

note Apple's Web site shows a fifth button, Genius, which recommends apps you might like based on the apps you already own. That feature does not appear to be implemented as of the first revision (version 3.2) of the iPad's operating system.

To view more information about an app, including screenshots and customer reviews, tap its icon.

tip It's sometimes difficult to get a sense of what an app offers by looking solely at screenshots, so be sure to tap the link that takes you to a developer's Web site for more information. Often companies will include video of how the app operates.

If you decide your life isn't complete without the app, tap the button that displays the price. The button changes to read "Buy App"; if the app is free, you'll see "Install App" (**Figure 2.2**). Tap it again to purchase, or tap anywhere outside the button to switch back to the price.

Figure 2.2
*Purchasing
an app*

Tap the price to reveal
the Buy App button.

After you enter your iTunes Store account password, the app downloads and is installed in the first open space on the Home screen (**Figure 2.3**).

Figure 2.3
The app appears on the Home screen and is automatically installed.

> **note** If you're connected to the Internet using 3G, large apps—over 20 MB—won't be downloaded. Connect to a Wi-Fi network or use iTunes on your computer and try the purchase again.

The App Store within iTunes on a computer

It may be more convenient to browse and purchase apps on your computer and then sync them to the iPad later. Fire up iTunes and click the iTunes Store item in the sidebar, and then click the App Store heading at the top.

As with the App Store on the iPad, you can browse featured and best-selling apps, poke through the categories, and search for specific titles. However, an extra step is required when buying apps in iTunes. After clicking the Buy App button, the app is downloaded and added to iTunes. When you next perform a sync, the app is automatically transferred to the iPad and appears on the Home screen.

Run iPhone apps on the iPad

You'll find apps that are written specifically for the iPad, but it can also run apps written for both the iPhone and iPod touch. In some cases, a single app can run on both devices—the developer includes the resources that take advantage of the iPad when run there, and ignores them when run on an iPhone or iPod touch.

Apps that have not been adapted to the iPad also work in one of two ways: either at their actual size centered in the screen, or enlarged to fill the screen (**Figure 2.4**).

Tap the 2x button in the bottom-right corner to scale the app to fill the screen, or tap the 1x button to return to the original size.

Figure 2.4
Resizing an iPhone app

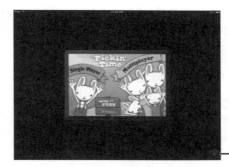

Tap to double size.

Tap to return to actual size.

Update Apps

When developers update their software, they submit changed versions to the App Store, where Apple approves the update and makes it available. Because everything goes through the App Store, your iPad can check for updates so you don't have to go searching for them online.

A numbered badge appears on the App Store icon in the Home screen indicating how many updates are ready to be downloaded. In iTunes, the badge appears on the Apps item in the sidebar (**Figure 2.5**).

Figure 2.5
App updates are available.

Badge on
App Store icon

Badge in iTunes

> **note** You don't have to wait for the iPad or iTunes to communicate with the Apple mothership. In the App Store app, tap the Updates button to trigger a check for new versions. In iTunes, select the Apps item in the sidebar and then click the Check for Updates button at the lower-right corner of the window.

To install the updates on the iPad, do the following:

1. Tap the App Store app to launch it.

2. Tap the Updates button in the bottom toolbar. A list of updated apps appears.

3. To learn more about the update, tap its name in the list. Otherwise, skip to the next step.

4. Tap the Free button next to any single app you want to download. When it changes to Install, tap it again.

   Or, tap the Update All button at the top of the screen to download and install all updates at once.

> **tip** A scary-looking dialog may appear before the download begins, warning you that an app may contain material inappropriate for children. Apple is strict about the type of content that's accepted into the App Store, so you shouldn't find anything too suggestive, and certainly nothing explicit. However, Apple can't control all content, especially for apps that fetch data from the Web, so the company throws up this disclaimer.

Remove Apps

As you download more apps—and I predict you will—you're going to find that some don't hold the allure they once did, or you discover a new app that does something better than the first one you downloaded. You can remove the app on the iPad itself, or disable it from syncing within iTunes.

On the iPad

1. Locate the app you want to remove on the Home screen, and then touch and hold its icon for a second. All of the apps begin to shake, and an X button appears.

2. Tap the X button (**Figure 2.6**).

3. Tap the Delete button in the confirmation dialog that appears.

Figure 2.6
*Remove an app
from the iPad.*

Delete button —

4. You can optionally rate the app, which will be reflected in its description at the App Store. Tap a star to give a rating between 1 and 5 and then tap the Rate button. Or, tap No Thanks to delete the app without rating it.

note The original apps that ship with the iPad cannot be removed. If they're in your way, consider moving them to another Home screen (described in "Customize the Home Screen," coming up).

In iTunes

1. Connect the iPad to your computer and select its name in the iTunes sidebar.

2. Click the Applications tab in the main section of the screen.

3. Locate the app you wish to remove, either in the list of applications or in the preview area of the different Home screens (**Figure 2.7**).

Figure 2.7
*Remove an app
in iTunes.*

4. Position your mouse pointer over the app you wish to remove and click the X button. Or, in the list, click the checkbox to the left so that it is not marked.

5. Click the Apply button to pass the changes along to the iPad. iTunes asks you to confirm that you want to remove the app, and if you click Yes, then the iPad is synced.

Share Apps

Apps you've downloaded can be loaded onto any other iPad, iPhone, or iPod touch that you sync with your computer. But what you may not know is that you can share apps with up to five other computers (including friends' computers) using the Home Sharing feature of iTunes.

For example, let's say I want to play a game of Scrabble for iPad with my wife. I've purchased the app, but she doesn't want to buy a new copy because she may not want to play it often. Here's how to get the app onto another device.

1. Make sure your friend's computer is on the same local network as your computer.

2. Enable Home Sharing in both computers by choosing Advanced > Turn On Home Sharing (if it's not already active).

3. Enter your iTunes account name (the email address you use for purchasing things from the iTunes Store) and password, and then click the Create Home Share button. Be sure to use the same account (yours, since you are sending the app) on both computers.

4. If iTunes asks to authorize the computer, click Yes. On your friend's computer, the name of your iTunes library appears in the sidebar.

5. Choose that library, click the disclosure triangle to the left of the name, and then click the Applications item.

6. Locate the app you want to transfer and drag it to the Library heading in the sidebar (**Figure 2.8**). The app file copies to your friend's iTunes library. He or she can then sync the iPad to install the app.

Figure 2.8
Share apps to a friend's computer.

Applications on your shared computer

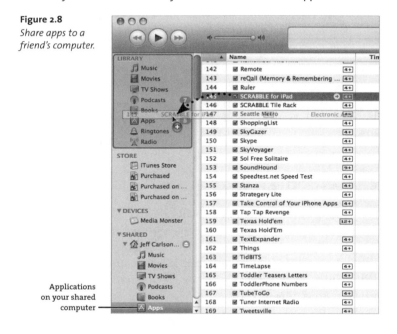

note   Because your friend didn't purchase the app originally, she needs to enter your iTunes password to update the app. If you trust your friend enough to give her your password, that's not a problem, but it also means she can buy anything from the iTunes Store on your dime.

Sharing Apps by Copying Files

The procedure I've just described is the outward-facing approach within iTunes, but you can also share apps by copying their files outside iTunes if you're comfortable doing that. Here's how:

1. Locate the app you want: In iTunes on a Mac, Control-click the app and choose Show in Finder. Under Windows, right-click the app and choose Show in Windows Explorer.

2. Copy the app file to the other computer over your network (or a USB memory stick, or whatever method you choose).

3. Drag the app file to the iTunes library on the other computer. That installs the app, ready for syncing to the iPad.

Set App Preferences

Every app has its own settings, but finding them can be scattershot. Many apps include preferences within the app itself, so you can do everything in one place. Apple's recommended (and awkward, in my opinion) method is to put preferences within the Settings app (**Figure 2.9**). Scroll to the bottom of the Settings screen to view apps, then tap an app's name to access its preferences.

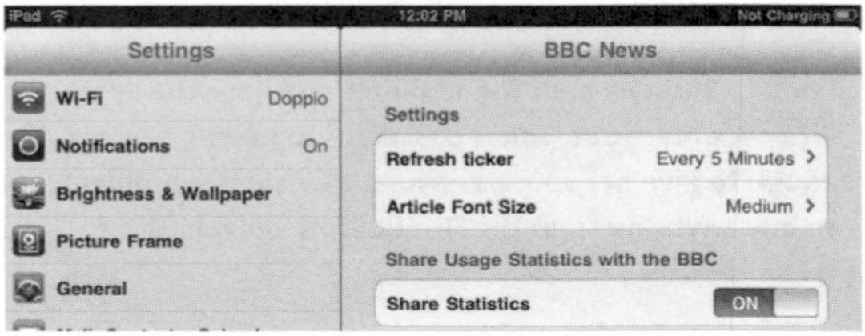

Figure 2.9
App-specific preferences in the Settings app

Enable Push Notifications

Some apps can take advantage of push notification, which is a way for data to arrive even when the iPad is in its sleep mode. For example, I use an app called Boxcar (boxcar.io) to notify me when someone sends a direct message via Twitter using a text alert, a sound, a badge, or all three.

note The built-in Mail app also uses push notifications—notifying you when new email messages arrive—but is configured elsewhere; see Chapter 4. The steps here apply to third-party apps that support notifications.

1. Go to Settings > Notifications.

2. If the feature is not yet enabled, tap the Notifications button to turn it On.

3. Tap the name of the app you wish to configure.

4. Tap the On/Off switches for the features you want: Sounds, Alerts, or Badges (**Figure 2.10**).

Figure 2.10
Choose push notification options.

5. Return to the Notifications screen or exit the Settings app to apply the changes.

Customize the Home Screen

I introduced the Home screen in Chapter 1 and mentioned how you can swipe each screenful of apps to find what you're looking for. What I didn't mention was that you can move the apps between screens, so you don't have to swipe several times to get a frequently-used app—very helpful since the iPad can have as many as 11 Home screens. It's also possible to change the background image to personalize your iPad.

On the iPad

1. Touch and hold any app for a second until the apps begin to shake.

2. Drag an app you want to move to a different position on the screen. Or, to move an app to another screen, drag it to the left or right edge of the screen and hold it there.

   After a moment, the screen advances and you still have control over positioning the app.

3. Lift your finger to drop the app in place.

4. Press the Home button to return to the Home screen's normal mode.

tip The apps in the Dock at the bottom of each Home screen remain the same, no matter which screen you're viewing. Put your most frequently used apps there.

In iTunes

1. Connect the iPad to your computer, select it in the sidebar, and go to the Apps tab.

2. Drag an app to a new location, including to other Home screens displayed in the right-hand column (**Figure 2.11**). (If the iPad is in its

wide orientation, the app screen thumbnails appear below the main screen.)

You can also drag an entire Home screen in that column to a different location. This is great if, for example, you keep games on one screen and business apps on another.

 Press Shift and click more than one app in the Applications tab to select several, and then drag them to a new Home screen all at once.

3. Click the Apply button to sync the changes to the iPad.

Figure 2.11
Drag an app to a new Home screen.

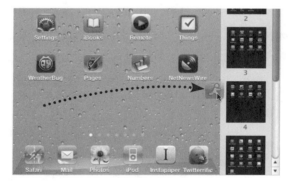

Change the Home screen image

The iPad includes many alternate Home screen images, or you can use one of your own photos as the background. You can also set the Lock Screen image.

1. Go to Settings > Brightness & Wallpaper.

2. Tap the Wallpaper button, which displays the current Lock and Home screen images.

3. Tap the next Wallpaper button to view images Apple includes with the iPad. Or, tap the Photo Library button or the name of one of your photo albums to view your images (**Figure 2.12**).

Figure 2.12
Choose an album of wallpaper images.

3. Tap an image to select it and to see a preview of how it will appear.

4. If the image is larger than the iPad's screen resolution (which includes most digital photos), you can refine its appearance. Resize it by using pinch and expand gestures, and reposition it by dragging with one finger.

5. Tap the Set Lock Screen, Set Home Screen, or Set Both button to make the change (**Figure 2.13**). Or, tap Cancel to choose a different image.

Figure 2.13
Set the wallpaper.

3

Browse the Web

I predict that within a year we won't be talking about how great it is to view Web pages on portable devices like the iPad. Web browsers on smartphones have always been pretty terrible. The iPhone demonstrated that it's possible to render a Web site that didn't need to be custom programmed to be readable on a mobile device. However, even that didn't prove to be 100 percent accurate, because although Safari *can* render a page as it would appear in a desktop Web browser, the screen size is still a limitation, leading many sites to adjust their code to accommodate.

The iPad is almost all screen, with a version of Safari that displays Web sites just as you'd see them on your Mac or PC. We won't wonder or marvel at how we get information online—we'll just get it.

Access Web Sites

Tap the Safari icon on the Home screen to launch the iPad's Web browser. I'm assuming you have an active Internet connection, either via Wi-Fi or 3G. If not, go back to Chapter 1 for a refresher on getting online.

 As soon as you try to access a Web site in Safari, the program checks for an Internet connection. If one isn't found, the iPad asks if you want to join a nearby Wi-Fi network.

Open and read a new Web page

Safari opens to a new blank page, with a layout similar to what you're accustomed to on your computer.

1. Tap the Address field.

2. Enter the address of the site you want to visit.

   To quickly erase what you've typed and start over, tap the cancel button (⊗) at the right edge of the Address field.

   As you type, Safari suggests matching URLs from your bookmarks or history in a popover (**Figure 3.1**).

 You don't need to type "http://" at the front of a URL in the Address field. Safari fills that in automatically.

3. Tap the Go key in the onscreen keypad or a suggested address in the popover. After a few seconds, the page appears.

 Safari builds its list of suggested sites based on browsing history and bookmarks (see "Create and Organize Bookmarks," later in this chapter).

Figure 3.1
*A new Safari
window*

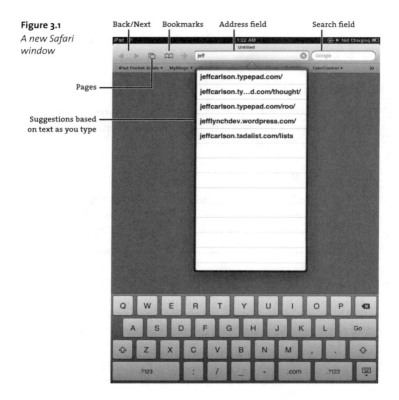

Back/Next   Bookmarks   Address field   Search field

Pages

Suggestions based
on text as you type

To read the site's content, flick or drag the page in any direction to scroll it. If you'd like to enlarge an area, double-tap that spot to zoom in—Safari smartly figures out how much zoom to apply based on the page's layout. You can also spread two fingers to enlarge manually. Double-tap or pinch to zoom back out.

tip   To quickly jump to the top of a Web page, tap the status bar at the top of the screen. (This shortcut works in most apps.)

To follow a link to another page, simply tap the text or image that is linked. You can return to the previous page by tapping the Back button in the toolbar.

Reload or cancel

Tap the icon at the right edge of the Address bar (🔄) to reload the page. While the content is downloading, the icon becomes a cancel button (⊗); tap it if you want to stop loading.

View your browsing history

What if you want to view a Web page you loaded yesterday? If you know the site's address, you could start typing it and pick it from the list of possible matches. Or, you could view the entire list of sites you've visited.

Safari and Flash

One area where Safari on the iPad differs from a Web browser on your computer is Flash: the iPad doesn't support Adobe's technology for playing movies, animations, and games. This omission is trumpeted as one of the iPad's failings, but honestly I see it as no big deal.

Although Flash is used to play back most of the video on the Web, it's just a delivery mechanism. Many sites, such as YouTube, now offer video using HTML5 code (which the iPad understands), and more sites are adding that capability.

More of an issue are popular online-only games in Flash, if you (or your kids) spend a lot of time playing them. But if the games are not available now, I suspect most will appear as iPad apps soon enough, or alternatives will crop up.

---

1. Tap the Bookmarks button in the toolbar.

2. Choose History in the popover that appears (**Figure 3.2**).

3. Tap the name of the site you visited. You may need to tap a date folder to locate it.

Figure 3.2
Viewing your browsing history

Tapping History views the folder's contents.

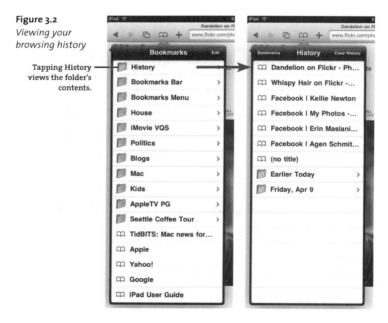

Open new pages

Unlike a Web browser in your Mac or Windows PC, Safari on the iPad does not let you view multiple Web sites in their own windows, or group them as tabs within one window. You can browse up to nine pages, however, one at a time, and switch between them. Do the following to open a new empty page.

1. Tap the Pages button in the toolbar to view the interface for managing open pages.

2. Tap the New Page placeholder (**Figure 3.3**). An empty Safari window appears, where you can enter a Web address or perform a search.

Figure 3.3
Opening a new page

Tap the New Page placeholder to open a blank window and keep the first page in memory.

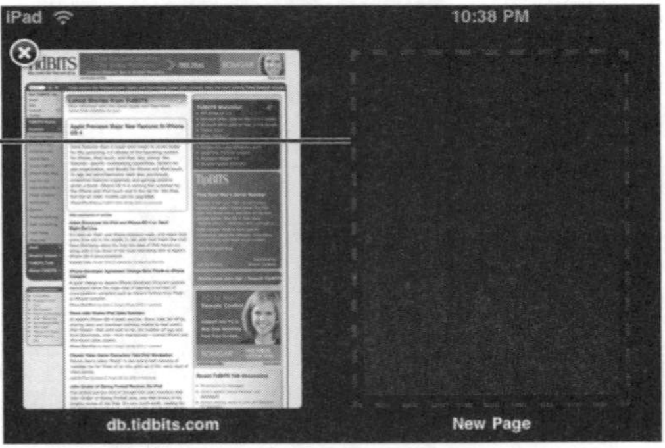

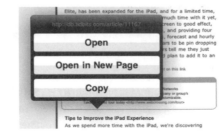

Another option is to open a link in a new page. Instead of just tapping the link, touch and hold it, and then tap Open in New Page (**Figure 3.4**).

Figure 3.4
Touching and holding a link

tip Bringing up the popover also reveals the link's URL and gives you the option to copy it to the iPad's memory for pasting elsewhere (such as in an outgoing Mail message).

With several pages open at the same time, switch between them by tapping the Pages button and then tapping the thumbnail of the page you wish to view.

Close pages

When you no longer wish to keep an open Web page, tap the Pages button and tap the X button in the upper-left corner of the page's thumbnail.

Watch videos

Many videos that appear on Web pages can be viewed within Safari (unless they're delivered using Flash; see the sidebar "Safari and Flash," earlier in the chapter). A play button appears on videos you can watch (**Figure 3.5**).

Figure 3.5
Embedded video

Button indicates you can play this video.

Tap the button to begin playing the video. When you do, the iPad's video controls appear (**Figure 3.6**).

Figure 3.6
Playing embedded video

VIDEO »   More Video | Multimedia »

Play/   Elapsed   Scrubber   Remaining   Full
Pause   time   bar   time   Screen

 tip   YouTube videos, even those that appear in embedded players on other sites' Web pages, get handed off to the YouTube app for playback.

The scrubber bar displays the video's progress; the light gray portion to the right of the playhead indicates how much of the video has been downloaded. To jump ahead in the movie, drag the playhead across the scrubber bar. Tap the Full Screen button to enlarge the video to use the entire iPad screen, hiding the rest of the Web page.

 tip   You can also use a two-fingered expand gesture (moving your fingers apart) on the movie to quickly zoom it into full-screen mode.

tip   In full-screen mode, double-tap the video to switch between viewing the full width of the movie (with black bars) or filling the screen (which crops the image). See Chapter 7 for more information about playing videos and other media.

Search the Web

What did we do before we could search the Internet for everything? How did we win trivia bets with our friends or recall specific movie quotes (and other important things, I'm sure)? You can navigate to any search engine's Web site, but it's easier to perform the search directly from the toolbar.

Tap the search field in Safari and start typing your search term (**Figure 3.7**). Tap the Search key in the onscreen keyboard or tap one of the suggested terms that appear as you type.

Figure 3.7
*Safari's
Search field*

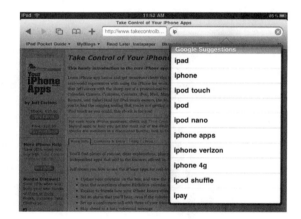

tip Safari uses Google as its default search engine, but you can also choose to set Yahoo as the source for the Search field. Go to Settings > Safari > Search Engine and choose Google or Yahoo.

note You're not limited to using just Google or Yahoo for searches. In addition to going to any search engine's Web site, several standalone search apps are available, such as Microsoft's Bing and, yes, even Google. They typically add other features not available in a Web browser; for example, you can speak a search term to the Google app, which deciphers what you said and delivers its results.

Create and Organize Bookmarks

A Web browser is a great reference tool, not just because there are more than 1 trillion Web pages on the Internet (Google's estimate in 2008), but because you can store bookmarks for sites that you want to visit later. Safari on the iPad can create bookmarks and also use the bookmarks you've created on your computer.

Open a bookmarked page

Apple includes a few basic bookmarks in Safari, which will give us a sense of how opening a bookmark works. Tap the Bookmarks button on the toolbar, and then tap the name of a Web page from the list to load it (**Figure 3.8**).

Figure 3.8
Choose a bookmark.

Here's a handy bookmark: Apple includes a Web version of the iPad User Guide at the bottom of the Bookmarks list.

Create a new bookmark

When you find a page you want to return to later, do the following:

1. Tap the **+** button in the toolbar.

2. In the popover that appears, tap the Add Bookmark button.

3. Edit the name of the bookmark, if you wish (**Figure 3.9**).

Figure 3.9
Create a bookmark.

4. Tap the button at the bottom of the popover and choose where the bookmark will be located in the Bookmarks hierarchy.

   Typically, there are just two levels to the hierarchy: the Bookmarks folder itself, and the Bookmarks Bar, a subfolder whose contents appear as clickable shortcuts beneath the toolbar. However, as I'll cover shortly, it's possible to import the bookmarks from your computer.

5. Tap the Save button to create the bookmark.

 I store nearly all of my active bookmarks on the Bookmarks Bar, organized in Safari on my Mac. For that reason, I choose to make the

Bookmarks Bar always visible in Safari (normally it appears only when you're typing in the Address or Search field). To do this, go to Settings > Safari and enabled the Always Show Bookmarks Bar option.

Edit a bookmark

Suppose you realize that your bookmark's name is too long to fit with other bookmarks on the Bookmarks Bar, or you want to put it into a different subfolder. Here's how to edit existing bookmarks on the iPad.

1. Tap the Bookmarks button on the toolbar.

2. Locate the bookmark you want to edit; this could mean tapping a subfolder (like Bookmarks Bar) to view its contents.

3. Tap the Edit button in the popover's navigation bar. The items in the list gain red icons to the left of their names (**Figure 3.10**).

Figure 3.10
Editing the Bookmarks list

4. Edit the bookmark in any of the following ways (**Figure 3.11**):

   ■ To reposition the item within the list, touch the icon at the far right and drag it to a new position.

   ■ Tap the bookmark name to change the title or URL. This is also where you can move the bookmark to another subfolder by tapping the button at the bottom of the popover. Use the navigation button at the top of the popover to return to the enclosing folder, or simply tap anywhere outside it to apply the change.

Figure 3.11
Editing a
bookmark

- To remove a bookmark, tap the red icon to the left of its name, which displays a Delete button to the right. Tap that Delete button to remove the bookmark. (This two-step process is designed to avoid accidentally deleting bookmarks.)

tip A faster method of deleting bookmarks (and many other things on the iPad, such as Mail messages), is to simply swipe left-to-right across the item's name to bring up the Delete button.

5. Tap the Done button to exit the editing mode.

note iTunes can synchronize bookmarks with the Mac or Windows version of Safari and with Internet Explorer 8 under Windows. I prefer this option not only because I keep the same bookmarks on both devices, but because it's easier to edit several bookmarks on the computer than on the iPad. See Chapter 9 for more information on syncing. Instructions for how to use Safari on the Mac can be found at support.apple.com/kb/HT3643; for Windows, see support.apple.com/kb/HT3657.

Add a Web page to the Home screen

Locating a bookmark in Safari's menus can require multiple steps. What if you want to jump to a frequently-viewed Web page more quickly? Create a Home screen icon for it.

1. In Safari, navigate to the page you want to bookmark.

2. Tap the **+** button.

3. Tap the Add to Home Screen button.

4. In the popover that appears, edit the icon's name (**Figure 3.12**).

5. Tap the Add button. The new icon appears on the Home screen.

    Tapping that icon opens the Web page in a new Safari window.

Figure 3.12
Creating a Home screen icon

Editing the name

Icon on Home screen

Share a page's address via email

You can easily share a Web page with someone by sending them a link via email. Tap the **+** button and choose Mail Link to this Page from the popover. A new outgoing email address appears with the page title already entered into the Subject field and the link in the body. All you have to do is enter a recipient's email address and tap Send.

Expand Safari's Capabilities with Bookmarklets

Safari supports JavaScript, a scripting language that offers all sorts of interactivity on the Web including bookmarklets, tiny bookmarks that use JavaScript code instead of a Web site address. What does that mean for non-developers? It adds features that Safari lacks.

For example, one of my favorite iPad and iPhone apps is Instapaper (www.instapaper.com). When I'm viewing a Web page that I want to read later—a long article, for example—I tap a "Read Later" book-marklet that Instapaper created in my Bookmarks Bar, which adds the page to my Instapaper account. Later, in Instapaper, I can read the page without being online, and in a format that strips out all the junk surrounding most Web pages (**Figure 3.13**).

Figure 3.13
The same article in Safari and Instapaper

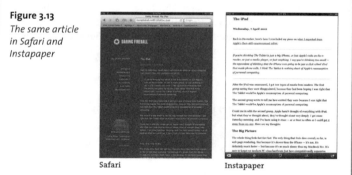

Safari   Instapaper

Another helpful bookmarklet is Find In Page (findinpage.blogspot.com), which lets you perform text searches within a Safari Web page. To find more, search for "bookmarklet" in your favorite search engine and explore.

AutoFill Forms

How many Web sites do you visit that require some sort of account? There's no way I can keep track of all the logins and passwords for various news, travel, and shopping sites. One option is to simply use the same password for everything, but that's dangerous. If someone were to discover that password, they'd have access to all of your sites.

Safari's AutoFill feature can keep track of those credentials for you, and give you the option of filling in the information with one tap.

tip **While we're talking about security, allow me to recommend 1Password (www.agilewebsolutions.com), a great secure repository for all of your logins and other sensitive information. 1Password exists as an application for the Mac and an app for the iPad/iPhone/iPod touch. On my Mac it's essential, letting me easily fill in logins and storing new logins as I create them. It can also keep my credit card information handy for when I'm making purchases. The mobile app can't tie directly into Safari (due to restrictions imposed by Apple on sharing data between apps), but it's very handy when I need to look up a login. The best part: if you have both, you can sync your logins between the computer and the device.**

Enable AutoFill

Before we start capturing passwords, we need to make sure AutoFill is turned on.

1. Go to Settings > Safari > AutoFill.

2. Toggle the switch for Names and Passwords to On.

3. If you want Safari to fill in personal information such as your name and address in forms, to save you from typing it all, enable the Use Contact Info option. Tap My Info to locate the entry for yourself in the Contacts app (see Chapter 9 for more information).

Store a new login

The first time you fill out a form, you have the option to save it.

1. When you tap a form field, the onscreen keyboard appears with buttons for jumping to the Previous or Next field (which is often easier than moving your fingers from the keyboard and tapping the next or previous field on the page), and for using AutoFill (**Figure 3.14**).

Figure 3.14
Filling in a form

Form buttons ————

2. Type the relevant information in the fields.

3. Tap the Go button in the onscreen keyboard, or tap the button that submits the data on the Web page (which may be labeled Submit, Log In, Go, or any number of other terse verbs).

4. In the dialog that appears, choose one of the following:

   - **Yes:** Save the password for later. The next time you visit, the name and password will automatically be filled in.

   - **Never for this Website:** Do not save the password, and never ask about saving it for this site in the future. I use this option when accessing sensitive sites such as my bank, where I'd prefer to manually enter the password each time.

   - **Not Now:** Ignore AutoFill for now, but allow Safari to ask you about it next time.

AutoFill contact information

When you encounter a form that asks for your personal information, tap one of the fields to bring up the keyboard and then tap the AutoFill button. The data from your Contacts entry appears (**Figure 3.15**).

Figure 3.15
Using AutoFill for contact information

AutoFill items appear with a yellow background.

Maintain Web Privacy

Safari's settings contain several options that are designed to limit how your data is used. Go to Settings > Safari and enable or disable the following options (**Figure 3.16**):

- **Fraud Warning:** If you follow a link to a site that's known to be a security risk, Safari gives you a warning and the option to continue.

- **JavaScript:** If you're concerned that a site may be using JavaScript to do something nefarious (like masquerade as a legitimate site), you can turn JavaScript off.

- **Accept Cookies:** By default, Safari only stores cookies—small bits of code that save some preferences or track your visit—created by sites you visit. You can also Never accept cookies or Always accept them.

Figure 3.16
Safari privacy settings

Security

Fraud Warning	ON

Warn when visiting fraudulent websites.

JavaScript	ON
Block Pop-ups	ON
Accept Cookies	From visited >
Databases	>

Clear History

Clear Cookies

Clear Cache

- **Clear History:** Tap this button to erase your entire browsing history.

 The Clear History feature is also available as a button in the navigation bar when you're viewing the History folder from the Bookmarks list.

- **Clear Cookies:** Tap this button to wipe out any stored cookies.

- **Clear Cache:** Safari stores the contents of recent Web pages so that if you return to a site, it doesn't need to re-download images and other data that may not have changed. If you see a Web page that doesn't seem to have changed its content, try clearing Safari's cache to force a reload.

note The Clear buttons erase all stored data; you can't go in and delete individual cookies as is possible in most desktop Web browsers, for example.

note The Databases option isn't really a privacy setting, but it's grouped with the other items. Tapping Databases reveals larger chunks of temporary data stored in Safari, like the iPad User Guide.

4

Communicate Using Mail

Email is a prime candidate for liberation from the desktop. A lot of what I do occurs via email, whether I'm corresponding with friends and relatives or tossing around ideas for upcoming projects. But there's no reason all of that has to happen in front of a computer. Even using a laptop can be a bother when all you want to do is check to see if someone replied to one of your messages.

Using the Mail app on the iPad, you can quickly read and reply to messages and dash off notes you may have otherwise ignored because of the hassle of doing it on the computer. Mail also handles incoming file attachments, making it a gateway for sending and receiving files wirelessly.

Set Up Mail

Most likely, you already have email accounts set up on the computer you use to sync with the iPad. You can also set up an account on the iPad itself—for example, you may want to use a MobileMe account on the iPad for personal mail that isn't synced to a work computer.

Sync mail accounts from a computer

Mail accounts you've set up in Mail on the Mac, or Outlook 2007, Outlook 2003, or Outlook Express under Windows appear in iTunes.

1. With the iPad connected to your computer, select its name in the sidebar and then click the Info tab (**Figure 4.1**).

Figure 4.1
*Mail accounts
listed in iTunes*

2. Click the checkbox for Sync selected Mail accounts, and then enable accounts you wish to access on the iPad.

3. Click the Sync button. The accounts' settings are added to the iPad's Mail app. Syncing transfers only the account settings, not any of the messages on your computer.

Set up an account on the iPad

If a mail account you want to use isn't set up on the computer you sync to, it's easy to add it directly on the iPad. Mail can automatically

configure accounts from MobileMe, Gmail, Yahoo Mail, and AOL, as well
as Microsoft Exchange accounts, provided you have your account name
and password.

> **note** The options on the iPad apply only to email accounts you've previously
> created. If you want to sign up for a new service, say a new Gmail
> account, you need to do that either on your computer or using Safari on the iPad.

1. Go to Settings > Mail, Contacts, Calendars.

2. Under the Accounts heading, tap the Add Account button.

3. Tap a service name that matches your account.

   If you get your email from a different provider, tap the Other button,
   and then tap the Add Mail Account button.

4. Enter a name for the account, the email address, and the password
   (**Figure 4.2**). The Description field automatically uses the address, but
   you can edit it separately if you prefer.

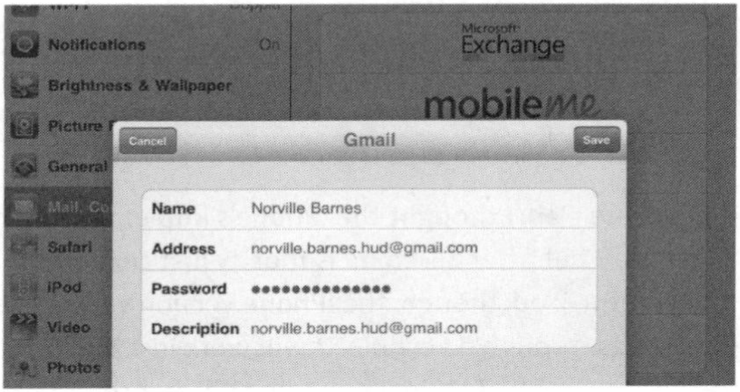

Figure 4.2
*Enter account
information.*

5. Tap the Save button. After the system verifies the information,
   the account appears in the Accounts list and you're done. You can

ignore the rest of the following steps. If, however, you're setting up a MobileMe account, tap the Next button.

If you're setting up an Other account, enter the account type (IMAP or POP) and the incoming and outgoing mail server information that your provider gave you when you signed up.

6. For MobileMe accounts, you can also set up over-the-air syncing of contacts, calendars, and bookmarks. Make any of those services available by tapping their On buttons. (See Chapter 9 for more on syncing personal information.)

tip This is a good opportunity to enable MobileMe's Find My iPad feature, which can locate the iPad on a map if you think it's lost or stolen. See Chapter 10 for more detail.

7. Tap the Save button to finish setting up the account.

tip If you're still having trouble configuring an account, check out this form from Apple to help you get the right information from your service provider: support.apple.com/kb/HT1277.

Read Messages

Before the iPad, I thought the iPhone's implementation of Mail was fine. Not great, but after all, email is mostly just text, right? Now that I've used Mail on the iPad, though, the iPhone version seems like I'm viewing my messages through a keyhole. It will work in a pinch, but the added screen real estate of the iPad makes a huge difference.

Mail presents two different views of your messages, depending on whether you're viewing the iPad in landscape or portrait orientation. The widescreen view displays mailboxes in a pane at left, with the currently-selected message at right (**Figure 4.3**).

Figure 4.3
Mail in landscape orientation

Active message ——

Unread message ——

The tall view displays only the current message. To browse messages one by one, tap the Previous and Next buttons (**Figure 4.4**). Or, to view and access other messages in the mailbox, tap the button at upper left, which is labeled with the name of the active mailbox. A popover containing the messages appears.

Figure 4.4
Mail in portrait orientation

Tap to view messages in mailbox.

Previous/Next message

tip

While reading a message, easily enlarge the body text by spreading two fingers in the reverse-pinch gesture.

As you read your email, Mail recognizes some data types and turns them into links. Tapping a Web address, as you might expect, opens the site in Safari. But Mail can also identify and act on street addresses, phone numbers, and email addresses. Tap an email address, and a new outgoing message is created. Tap a street address, and the Maps app launches and shows you the location.

You can also choose how to interact with the data. Tap and hold a link and then choose an option from the popover that appears (**Figure 4.5**).

Figure 4.5
Acting on a link in a message

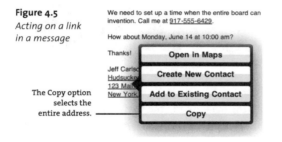

The Copy option selects the entire address.

Tap the Details link in the upper-right corner of a message to reveal the To and Cc fields, which are otherwise hidden. (You can also make sure they're visible by default; go to Settings > Mail, Contacts, Calendars > and set the Show To/Cc Label switch to On.) Showing details also presents the Mark as Unread option, which I often tap after reading an important message to make sure I see the email later when I'm catching up on my computer.

View information about senders and recipients

In its attempt to shield people from complexity, Apple chose to show email senders and recipients as friendly named blobs instead of addresses like "norvile.barnes.hud@gmail.com". Those blobs become useful buttons, however.

Tap any sender or recipient to view more information (**Figure 4.6**). If the person is not in your list of contacts, you can easily add them by tapping the Create New Contact button. The popover changes to let you edit contact information; tap Done to add the person to your Contacts list. Or, tap Add to Existing Contact if this is a different address for someone you already know.

On the other hand, tapping the button of a person already in your address book displays all of their information. That makes it easy to tap their address to view the location in the Maps app, for example.

Figure 4.6
Viewing sender information

Add the sender to your Contacts list, or add the address to an existing contact.

A new sender   Someone you already know

> **tip** Viewing information about a sender or recipient also reveals a neat shortcut. Say you want to send a friend the contact information of someone else you know. Instead of opening to the Contacts app, you can do it from within Mail. Locate a message from—or addressed to—the person whose information you want to share. Tap the person's name. In the popover that appears, scroll to the bottom of the information and tap the Share Contact button. A new outgoing message is created with the contact's information stored in a Vcard (.vcf) file as an attachment. When your friend receives the email, he can add the Vcard file to his contact-management software.

Navigate accounts and mailboxes

It's not unusual for someone to have more than one email account. The interface for accessing them all isn't obvious, however. Use the controls in the navigation bar that appears either at the top of the left-hand pane (landscape orientation) or at the top of the popover (portrait orientation).

1. Starting at the Accounts list, tap the name of an account (**Figure 4.7**).

2. Tap a mailbox, such as Inbox, to open it.

3. Tap the message you want to read.

Figure 4.7
*Navigating an
account hierarchy*

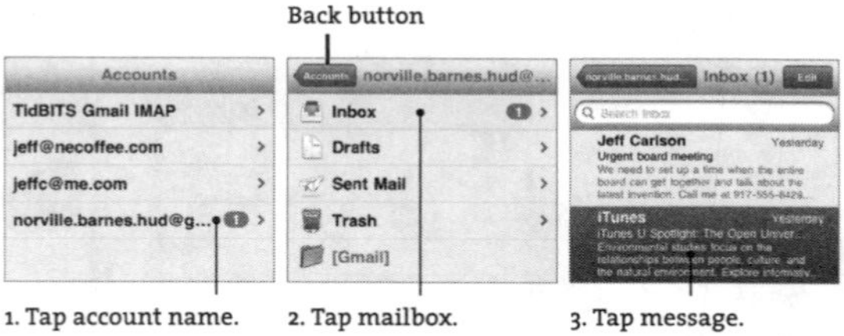

Back button

1. Tap account name.　2. Tap mailbox.　3. Tap message.

You can always go back in the hierarchy by tapping the back button. If you're going from one Inbox and want to view another account's Inbox, you need to tap back to the Accounts list, choose the other account, and drill down from there.

> **tip** To preview more of each message in the mailbox list, go to Settings > Mail, Contacts, Calendars, tap the Preview button, and choose up to five visible lines of text.

> **tip** Although you may have hundreds (or thousands!) of messages in a mailbox, Mail keeps the list trim by showing only the 50 most recent items. To view up to 200 messages, go to Settings > Mail, Contacts, Calendars and tap the Show button. You're given the choice of viewing 25, 50, 75, 100, or 200 recent messages in any given account.

Changes in Mail under iPhone OS 4

iPhone OS 4, which at the time of this writing is scheduled for release in Fall 2010, brings many changes to the Mail app. The next version of Mail introduces one unified Inbox to collect the contents of all accounts' Inboxes. Or, if you want to keep accounts separate, a fast Inbox switching feature saves the repetition of tapping repeatedly to exit and enter accounts to reach their mailboxes. Also new will be the capability to set up multiple Exchange accounts—currently you can have just one at a time.

Check for new mail

When the iPad is connected to the Internet, it can check for new messages, even when Mail isn't the active app, using two methods: Push, where new messages are delivered to Mail as soon as they're available; and Fetch, where Mail contacts each accounts' server to see if there are any new messages. Of course, you can also perform a manual check whenever you want.

Check mail manually

Opening the Mail app triggers a check for new messages, so that's usually all you need to do. If you're eagerly awaiting a response from someone, you can also tap the Refresh button (🔄) at the bottom of the side panel or popover to load new mail.

Get new mail using Push

Push is available for MobileMe, Exchange, and Yahoo accounts. Do the following to enable it:

1. Go to Settings > Mail, Contacts, Calendars.

2. Tap the Fetch New Data button.

3. Make sure the Push option is set to On.

Generally, Push applies to all of your accounts that support the feature. However, it's possible to disable Push for some accounts: On the same Fetch New Data screen above, tap the Advanced button, tap an account name, and then choose the Fetch or Manual option instead of Push.

Check mail on a schedule

For accounts that can't use Push, you can specify an interval for when Mail does its check, which happens in the background no matter which app is running or if the iPad is asleep.

1. Go to Settings > Mail, Contacts, Calendars.

2. Tap the Fetch New Data button.

3. Tap a time interval to select it (**Figure 4.8**). If you choose Manually, the accounts are only checked when you open Mail or tap the Refresh button.

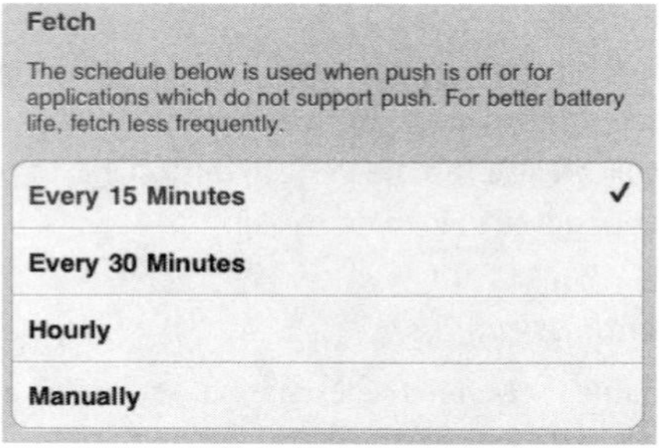

Figure 4.8

Specify how often Mail checks for new messages.

Fetch

The schedule below is used when push is off or for applications which do not support push. For better battery life, fetch less frequently.

Every 15 Minutes ✓

Every 30 Minutes

Hourly

Manually

note Since the iPad is a mobile device, it's likely you could be checking mail using the 3G network connection or on a Wi-Fi network that doesn't belong to you, like at a coffee shop. If you're concerned about securing the Internet connection, see Chapter 10 to learn how to set up a VPN (virtual private network).

When new mail arrives, the Mail icon on the Home screen appears with a badge indicating the total number of unread messages in all accounts. The mailbox navigation button within Mail also displays an unread message count, although the number applies only to that mailbox (**Figure 4.9**).

Figure 4.9
New mail indicators

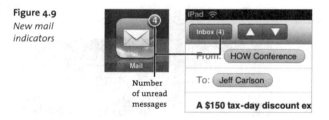

Number of unread messages

View file attachments

Although email isn't the most effective delivery mechanism for sending files, people frequently attach documents to messages. Mail on the iPad does a good job of handling the most common types of files you're likely to encounter, such as images, PDF files, and Microsoft Word, among others.

A file attachment is included in the body of a message (**Figure 4.10**, on the next page). The appearance of the attachment depends on the file's type and size:

- Images generally appear unaltered, as long as Mail can preview the format.

- Large files are not automatically downloaded, and appear with a dotted outline and generic download icon.

- A file that Mail cannot display within the message body shows up as an icon containing the file name and size.

Figure 4.10
File attachments

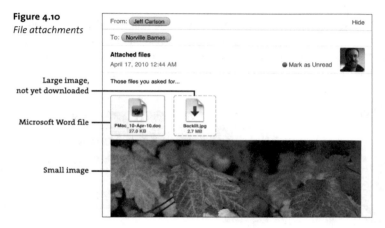

Large image, not yet downloaded

Microsoft Word file

Small image

To preview or open an attachment, do the following:

1. Tap the icon to see a full screen preview (if Mail can read it), which Apple calls Quick Look.

2. In the preview, tap the Open In button in the upper-right corner of the screen. A popover lists which apps can work with the file; tap one to launch the app and open the file. (If the button doesn't appear, there is no software installed that can read the file.)

 If a compatible app is installed, the file attachment icon reflects that app's document format, so it's usually easy to tell right away whether you can open an attachment.

You can also access those options directly without first viewing the Quick Look preview. Touch and hold the icon until a popover appears with options to open in a compatible app or to choose another (**Figure 4.11**).

tip Apps must be written to run on the iPad in order to take advantage of the capability to open file attachments. Mail doesn't recognize apps that run only on the iPhone or iPod touch.

Figure 4.11
Choose how to view or open the attachment.

Compose Messages

If only we could sit back in lounge chairs, feet propped on a table, and read email all day long like the people in Apple's iPad commercials. Alas, email demands interaction, so at some point you'll find yourself writing new messages and replying to existing ones.

Create a new message

In Mail, do the following:

1. Tap the New Message button (🖊). An empty message appears.

2. In the To field, begin typing the name of the person you want to send the email to. Mail displays a list of possible contacts (**Figure 4.12**, on the next page); tap one to enter it.

You can also tap the Add (⊕) button to view a popover containing all your contacts; scroll or use the Search field to locate the person you want.

Figure 4.12
List of suggested mail recipients

> **tip**   You can type any aspect of a person's name or email address to find a match; you don't need to always begin with the correct address or person's first name.

3. If you want to copy other people on the message, tap the Cc/Bcc, From field. Enter addresses into the Cc (carbon copy) or Bcc (blind carbon copy) fields.

   If you prefer to send the message from another account, tap the From field and choose one from the popover that appears.

> **tip**   Mail's preferences include an option to specify a default outgoing account (go to Settings > Mail, Contacts, Calendars, tap the Default Account button, and select one of your accounts). However, the setting applies only when you're creating new messages in other apps, such as when you send a link to a Web page in Safari. When you create a new message in Mail, the message is addressed as coming from whichever account you're currently viewing.

4. Tap the Subject field and enter a short title or summary. (Don't leave it blank; many mail servers flag messages with empty Subject lines as spam.)

5. Type your message into the main field (**Figure 4.13**).

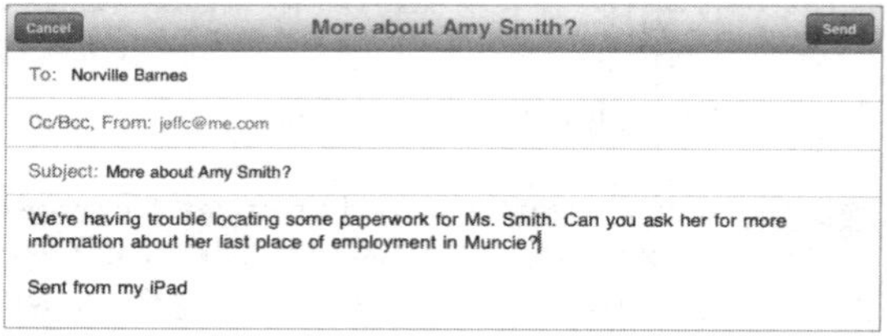

Figure 4.13
*Writing the
email message*

Cancel	More about Amy Smith?	Send

To: Norville Barnes

Cc/Bcc, From: jeflc@me.com

Subject: More about Amy Smith?

We're having trouble locating some paperwork for Ms. Smith. Can you ask her for more information about her last place of employment in Muncie?

Sent from my iPad

6. When you're finished, tap the Send button.

If you're not ready to dispatch the message, tap the Cancel button and then tap Save to store the email in the Drafts folder for editing and sending later.

note Outgoing messages have the text "Sent from my iPad" appended to the end, a bit of text called a signature. You can change the text in Mail's preferences. Go to Settings > Mail, Contacts, Calendars and tap the Signature button. Edit the text to whatever you like, then apply the change by returning to the Mail, Contacts, Calendars screen.

tip Mail's messages can handle more than just text, as I mentioned when talking about opening file attachments earlier. For outgoing messages, for example, this means you could copy a block of content on a Web page in Safari—with its text formatting and graphics—and paste it into a Mail message.

Reply to a message or forward it

When a message requires a response, reply to the sender by doing the following:

1. With a message open, tap the Reply/Forward button (⬅).

2. Tap Reply in the popover that appears. A new outgoing message is created, with the contents of the previous method quoted at the bottom of the message area.

3. Type your reply and then tap Send.

tip When you reply or forward a message, the entire referenced message is quoted. Often it's better to include just one relevant line or paragraph that you're responding to. Before tapping the Reply/Forward button, select the range of text to quote; only that section appears (Figure 4.14).

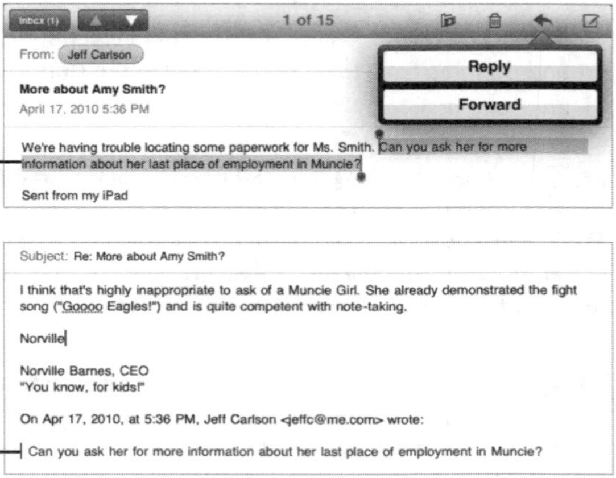

Figure 4.14
Replying with
selected text

Selected text ——

Text quoted in reply ——

note There's no way to attach a file in an outgoing message within Mail. That doesn't mean attachments aren't possible, though. You just need to do it from whichever app has the content you wish to share via email. For example, in the Photos app you can share a photo by email, which creates a new outgoing mail message with the photo already attached.

Manage Messages

It doesn't take long before email starts to pile up, and even though it's not the same as a foot-high stack of paper letters, I find there's a psychic drain when confronting an Inbox with hundreds of messages. Mail on the iPad doesn't have the same depth of features for managing email that you'll find in a desktop application, but it does let you delete, file, and search for messages.

Delete a message

Unless you're an obsessive archivist, don't try to keep every message that comes your way. To delete a message after you've read it, tap the Delete (🗑) button in the toolbar. The message is moved to the account's Trash folder.

Even better, you don't need to read a message to delete it. When you're viewing the contents of a mailbox and see a message that's clearly undesirable (yes, I get a lot of spam, can you tell?), do this: swipe one finger across the item from the left or the right. Then tap the Delete button that appears (**Figure 4.15**).

Figure 4.15
Swipe to delete.

Swipe across. ⎯⎯⎯

⎯⎯ Tap to delete.

Dealing with Email Spam

Unfortunately, the Mail app doesn't offer any help with unsolicited junk mail, making the iPad less desirable as one's primary destination for email. However, you don't need to be an IT administrator to cut down the amount of spam that reaches your Inbox. Most Internet service providers offer spam filtering at the server level, so a lot of the dreck out there gets trapped before it reaches your iPad.

Move a message

To keep a message but get it out of the way in your Inbox, file it in another folder within your account.

1. With the message open, tap the Move button (📁).

2. Tap a mailbox in the Mailboxes list in the sidebar to move the message there (**Figure 4.16**).

Figure 4.16
Moving a message

Delete or move multiple messages

Sending messages to the Trash or to other mailboxes one-by-one will make you crazy if there are many to process. Instead, delete or move them in batches.

1. Display the contents of a mailbox, either by tapping its name in the toolbar in portrait orientation or by turning the iPad to landscape orientation.

2. Tap the Edit button in the navigation bar.

3. Tap the messages you wish to delete or move. The ones you select gain a red checkmark and appear in a stack to the right (**Figure 4.17**).

Figure 4.17
Process multiple messages

Selected messages

Delete and
Move buttons

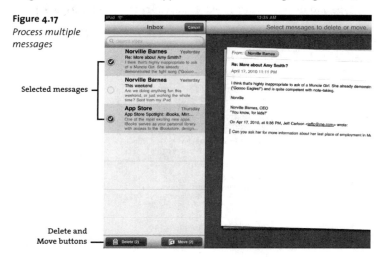

4. Tap the Delete or Move button at the lower-left corner of the mailbox. Or, tap the Cancel button at the top if you change your mind.

Search for messages

A powerful tool in managing piles of email is the capability to find something quickly by performing a search. In this respect, Mail provides some help, though I'm hoping for more in the future.

1. Go to the mailbox you want to search and then tap the Search field.

2. Tap a button to specify which portion of the messages should be searched: the From field, the To field, the Subject field, or All.

 That's right, there's no option to search the *contents* of your messages, which boggles my mind. I hope the capability arrives in iPhone OS 4.

3. Type a term in the Search field. Results appear in the list (**Figure 4.18**).

4. Tap a message to read it.

Figure 4.18
Searching a mailbox

Mail initially looks through the messages that have been downloaded to the iPad. If you don't find what you're looking for, tap the Continue

Search on Server option at the bottom of the list to query the mail server for more results.

tip   Another limitation of Mail's built-in search is that you can only peer into one mailbox at a time. There's a better way, however. Go to the Home screen and perform a Spotlight search instead (Figure 4.19). You'll get results from every searchable app, but it's easy enough to scroll down to the Mail messages, which are pulled from all mailboxes.

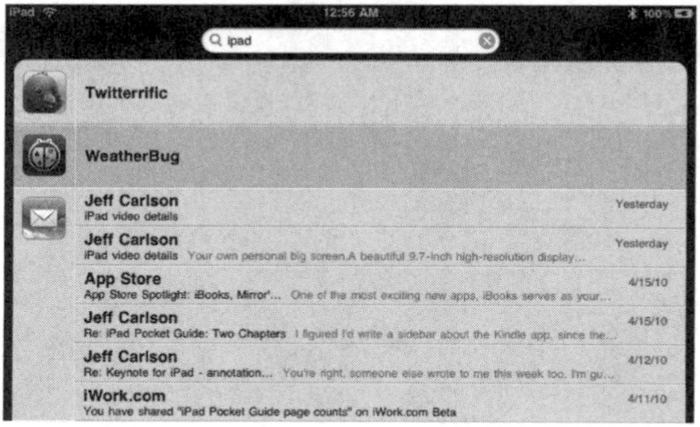

Figure 4.19
Search results using Spotlight

Other Text Correspondence

Email isn't the only method of corresponding on the iPad. I also use AIM for iPad (products.aim.com/products/ipad) to occasionally chat with people who use AOL Instant Messenger or iChat on the Mac. Being a third-party app, it can't receive messages in the background, but it's great for asking a quick question of friends online.

I also frequently keep up with Twitter using Twitterrific for iPad (twitterrific.com/ipad). Several other Twitter clients are available, too, so try them out and see which one is your favorite.

5

View Photos

Just *look* at that screen! Full color, high resolution, larger than a phone, attached to a device that's more comfotable to hold than a laptop. If the iPad didn't already do a thousand other things, you'd think it was designed solely for displaying digital photos.

When you have an iPad stocked with your favorite photos, you have a portable presentation machine. Maybe you want to show off your latest snapshots. Maybe you're a photographer (or real estate agent, or designer, or...) showing a portfolio to a prospective client. Maybe you want to store photos on the iPad while on vacation instead of toting a laptop. Maybe you need to display a slideshow using a projector or on an HDTV. Or maybe you just want to be able to look at your favorite photos whenever you feel like it. The Photos app can deliver your images.

Getting Photos onto the iPad

Where are your photos coming from? You have four options: sync photos from your computer; import photos directly from a camera or memory card using an adapter; send photos to an email account you check on the iPad; or copy pictures from Web pages in Safari.

Sync photos from the computer

With most photos now being captured digitally, it's likely you use photo-management software to keep track of them all. Or, you might prefer to organize the image files in a folder on disk. iTunes can handle both.

Sync with photo management software

iTunes recognizes libraries in iPhoto 4.0.3 or later and Aperture 3.0.2 or later on the Mac, and Photoshop Elements 3.0 or later for Windows.

1. Connect the iPad to the computer, open iTunes, and select the iPad in the sidebar.

2. Click the Photos tab.

3. Enable the Sync Photos from option and choose your photo software from the pop-up menu (**Figure 5.1**).

4. To transfer your entire library, choose the first option: All photos, albums, events, and faces.

   Or, enable the second radio button and then mark the checkboxes of any albums, events (or projects, in Aperture), or faces.

note The option to group photos based on events/projects or faces is supported only if you're syncing with iPhoto or Aperture. If you're using Photoshop Elements in Windows, you get the option of syncing all photos and albums or specifying selected albums.

Figure 5.1
*Photos pane
in iTunes*

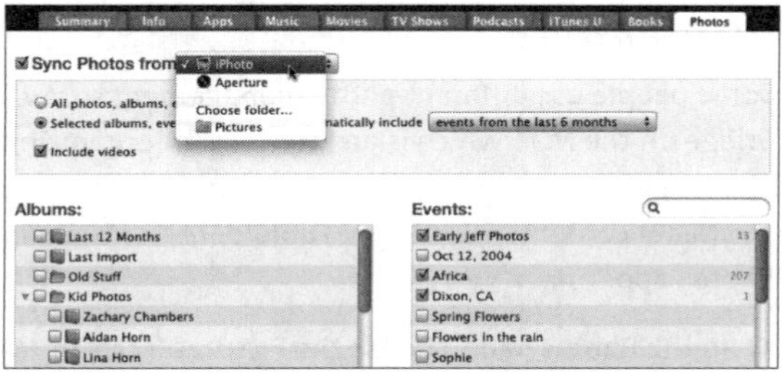

Using the radio button's pop-up menu, you can make some items appear automatically. For example, regardless of which checkboxes are selected in the Events or Projects list, you can choose to have the photos from all events from the last month appear on the iPad.

5. Top copy video files located in your library, mark the Include videos checkbox.

6. Click the Sync button. iTunes optimizes the photos and transfers them to the iPad.

Just What Does Optimizing Do to Photos?

When you sync photos, iTunes resizes them to 1,536 pixels on the shortest side. So, for example, a vertical shot could be something like 1,536 pixels wide by 2,048 pixels tall, while a horizontal shot would be 2,048 by 1,536 pixels.

It also converts them to JPEG format, which applies compression to further reduce the file size. Those are still respectable dimensions, enabling you to zoom in and retain detail, and it's unlikely you'll see any noticeable image degradation.

Sync with a folder

Some people use different photo management software such as Adobe Bridge on the Mac, which is an interface for organizing and viewing photos in folders, or prefer to manage the files by hand. iTunes can use the folder contents—including subfolders—as the media source for the Photos app.

1. In the Photos pane, choose the Pictures (Mac) or My Pictures (Windows) default locations. Or, click Choose folder and specify a different folder.

2. To include everything in the folder, choose the All folders option. Or, click the Selected folders button and mark the checkboxes for the folders you wish to sync in the Folders list (**Figure 5.2**).

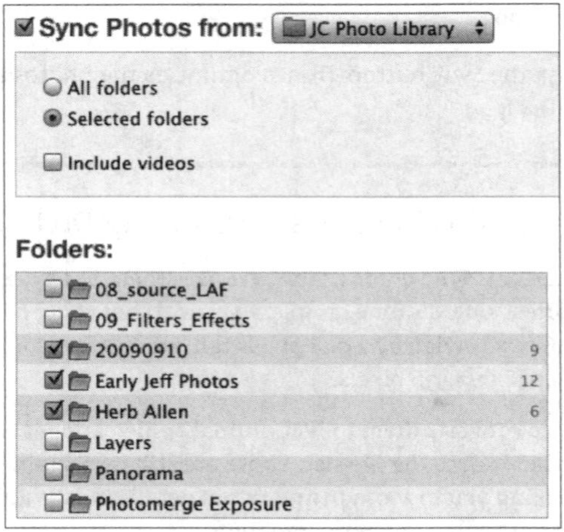

Figure 5.2
Sync photos from subfolders.

3. Click the Sync button to start the transfer.

tip The iTunes interface is a little confusing on this part. In the example above, the only photos transferred are the ones in the selected folders (27 pictures). What's not synced are the photos in the parent folder, "JC Photo Library". If I wanted just the images in that folder, and none of the images from the subfolders, I'm out of luck: I'd get either the contents of specific subfolders (Selected folders option) or everything in "JC Photo Library," subfolders included (All folders option). So, if you're going to organize photos at the folder level, I recommend storing image files in subfolders, not parent folders.

Make an Instant Photo Portfolio

I know photographers who are asking themselves: Do I buy a new lens, or buy an iPad and have an awesome portable portfolio? For the latter, here's a quick way to build an updated portfolio of good images.

1. In iPhoto, Aperture, or Photoshop Elements for Windows, create a smart album that collects your top-ranked photos. For example, in iPhoto choose File > New Smart Album, give it a name, and set the parameter pop-up menus to read "My Rating is greater than four stars". Click OK.

2. In iTunes, click the Photos tab and make sure that smart album is enabled in the Albums list.

3. Click the Sync button to transfer those photos.

As you add new high-ranked photos to your library, they automatically appear on the iPad the next time you sync.

Import photos from a camera

Using Apple's optional iPad Camera Connection Kit, you don't need iTunes as a middleman for your photos. The kit includes two adapters that connect to the iPad's dock connector: one that accepts SD memory cards and one that accepts a standard USB cable.

tip Wait, did I just say that the iPad can gain a regular USB port? Yes...but there are strings attached. The iPad uses the USB camera connector for transferring image and video files only—but there are a couple of surprises, too. Plug in a USB headset to listen to audio or use a headset's microphone. The benefit of this approach over plugging iPhone-compatible headphones into the iPad's headphone port is the capability to use higher-quality audio electronics. For example, I own a Sennheiser headset that's normally connected to my Mac for Skype calls; I can do the same (using the Skype app) on my iPad now. The other surprise is that the connector recognizes some USB keyboards, which is great if you don't own the iPad Keyboard Dock or a Bluetooth wireless keyboard.

To import photos via a camera adapter, do the following:

1. Plug one of the adapters into the iPad.

2. Insert an SD card or plug in a USB cable connected to your camera, depending on which adapter you're using. If the latter, turn on the camera's power.

tip To transfer photos directly from an iPhone, connect the iPhone's sync cable to the USB connector. (Unfortunately, the iPad can't charge the iPhone's battery over this connection, which would be cool in a pinch.)

3. Unlock the iPad. The Photos app opens and displays the photos on the card or camera.

4. To import all photos, skip to the next step.

   If you'd rather import just some of the images, tap the ones you want; a blue checkmark indicates the ones you've selected (**Figure 5.3**).

5. Tap the Import All button to begin copying the files.

If you made selections, tap the Import button, which brings up a popover with options to Import All (overriding your selections, in case you changed your mind at the last minute) or Import Selected. Tap one to begin copying the images to the iPad.

Click the Stop Import button if you want to halt the transfer; doing so doesn't remove any selections you made before importing.

Figure 5.3
Selecting photos for import

6. When importing is complete, you're given the option to delete or keep the images on the camera or SD card. I advise tapping Keep, and then erasing the card later using the camera's format controls.

7. Remove the SD card or turn off the camera. The transferred photos appear in a new album called Last Import.

tip Photos imported directly from a camera or card can be deleted later by viewing the image and tapping the Trash button (🗑). Tap the Rotate button (↻) to turn the picture 90 degrees counter-clockwise if necessary.

Import photos from email

Do you have a family member who likes to send photos via email? Rather than dig through your old messages to view those photos later, add them to the iPad's photo collection.

1. In the Mail app, open the message containing the photo attachments.

2. Touch and hold a photo to bring up a popover containing actions you can take (**Figure 5.4**).

Figure 5.4
*Saving images
from Mail*

3. Tap the Save Image button. Or, if several images are included, tap the Save *[number]* Images button. The photos are added to the Saved Photos album in the Photos app.

Import photos from other apps

The ability to save images from Mail also applies to other apps. In Safari, for example, touch and hold any image and then tap Save Image to store it. However, keep in mind that images on the Web don't have the same high resolution as ones you'd import from your camera, so they may not appear as good when expanded to fill the iPad's screen.

tip What if I told you it's possible to add a camera to the iPad, no soldering iron needed? Headlight Software's Camera for iPad connects wirelessly to an iPhone running the same software, using the iPhone's camera as input. Take a shot on the iPhone and it's delivered to the iPad. There's even an option to use the iPad as a big fill flash!

View Photos

We've covered all the ways to get photos onto the iPad, but that's just preamble for viewing them.

View a photo

Open the Photos app and tap the Photos button at the top of the screen to see thumbnails all of the photos stored on the iPad. Tap a photo to open it (**Figure 5.5**).

Figure 5.5
A photo viewed widescreen

The onscreen controls disappear after a few seconds so you can enjoy just the image. Rotate the iPad to match the photo's orientation for the best effect.

While viewing an image, you can do a number of things:

- Tap once anywhere to make the controls reappear. Tap again to make them go away again, or wait a few seconds.

- Double-tap anywhere on the photo to zoom in. Double-tapping again zooms back out to fit

- To zoom further in, with more control, pinch two fingers outward. Swipe anywhere on the image to view a different area of the photo. To zoom back out, pinch two fingers together or double-tap the screen.

- To quickly skim all of the photos, tap once to view the controls and then drag the navigation bar at the bottom of the screen (**Figure 5.6**). The preview is extremely fast because the Photos app displays low-resolution images as you drag, giving you a sense of what the photo is without having to draw all of the detail. If you pause, the higher-resolution version appears.

Figure 5.6
Quickly navigating photos

Drag along strip.

- Tap the All Photos button at the top left corner to return to the Photos pane and the grid of your images.

View collections

In addition to the big free-for-all that is the Photos pane, your images are also organized into collections. These can be albums, events, or faces, depending on the software on your computer. Each type is a different way of categorizing the photos, but the controls are the same.

1. Tap the Albums, Events, or Faces button to switch to that pane (if the option is available).

2. Pinch outward with two fingers on a collection you want to open. As you do so, the photos within unstack themselves so you can preview what you're about to open (**Figure 5.7**). If it's not the set you were expecting, just pinch your fingers together to return the collection to its stacked state.

Figure 5.7
Previewing a collection

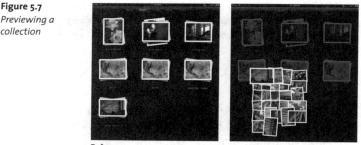

Before   Pinched outward

3. When you've expanded a collection far enough, it takes over the entire screen. Tap a photo thumbnail to view the image.

tip You know, I'm a big fan of useless shortcuts, things that were implemented just because they could be. And here's a great one. Instead of just tapping a thumbnail to view the photo full screen, use the expanding pinch gesture to enlarge it. Now, before you let go, *rotate your fingers*. The image can be freely rotated and scaled as long as your fingers are touching the glass. Why? I couldn't tell you. Maybe so you could preview a landscape photo in portrait orientation without rotating the iPad. Or maybe because the graphics capabilities inside the iPad can do it, and that's good enough reason. I don't know, but it's fun to play with.

tip I think this one is my favorite Photos tip: Instead of trying to tap the back button in the upper-left corner of the screen (which is labeled with the name of the enclosing folder), pinch two fingers together to collapse the stack you're currently viewing. It's much faster because your fingers are likely already in place from opening a stack or zooming in on an image.

tip To change the photo used for someone's Faces collection, go to iPhoto or Aperture and switch to the Faces view. Move your mouse pointer over the person's image to preview their photos, and find one you want. If you're in iPhoto, double-click the photo to view all photos associated with that name; if you're in Aperture, you don't need to take that extra step. Next, right-click or Control-click the photo and choose Set Key Photo. Sync again to apply the change.

View photos in Places

The Photos app offers one more type of collection that works a bit differently than the others. A Places pane appears if any of your images include location tags—GPS coordinates marking where the photos were shot, either written to the file when captured (the iPhone can do this, as can some GPS add-on devices for some cameras) or applied in iPhoto, Aperture, Photoshop Elements, or other software.

When you tap the Places button, you see a map that features red pins marking where photos were taken. Tap a pin to view a stack (**Figure 5.8**). As with other collections, pinch or tap the stack to view its photos.

Figure 5.8
*Photos with
location
information*

Location pin —

Play a video

Most digital cameras now shoot video as well as stills, so the Photos app can play video, too. In iTunes, makes sure you enable the Include videos option in the Photos pane. The iPad Camera Connection Kit also allows you to import videos you've shot directly into the iPad. Some cameras' video may not play, though; footage from my Flip MinoHD won't play on the iPad, but I can transfer them intact to my computer later. When you come across a video clip in the Photos app, do any of the following:

- Tap the Play button that appears in the middle of the screen to start playing. Or, you can tap the Play button in the toolbar (**Figure 5.9**).

- Touch and hold the playhead to skim through the filmstrip and locate a particular section of the video. If you hold for a moment, the filmstrip spreads out horizontally to give you finer control while skimming.

- While the video is playing, tap the pause button (■) to stop playback.

Figure 5.9
*Viewing
video clips*

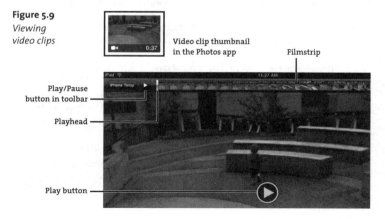

Video clip thumbnail
in the Photos app

Filmstrip

Play/Pause
button in toolbar

Playhead

Play button

 tip   A video in the Photos app benefits from the photo controls, which
means you can pinch to zoom a video while it's playing.

Here's a cool side effect of playing videos in the Photos app. Using the iPad Camera Connection Kit, you can import movies—the Hollywood kind— and watch them on the iPad. For example, if you're going on vacation and don't want to bring a laptop, but the number of movies you want to watch wouldn't fit on the iPad's internal storage, load up some inexpensive SD memory cards. Using a program such as Handbrake (www.handbrake.fr) on your computer, digitize your DVDs to digital .m4v files. Copy those to one or more SD memory cards, then insert one into the memory card adapter. Transfer a movie to the iPad in the Photos app and then watch it there. (It won't show up in the Videos app.) When you're done, delete the movie and transfer another one.

View a Slideshow

Swiping is fine for showing off a few pictures, but there are times when you'll want the iPad to drive a photo presentation. In that case, set up an impromptu slideshow of one of your albums (such as the smart album-based portfolio I mentioned in the sidebar earlier in the chapter).

1. Open a collection in any of the panes, or go to the Photos pane if you want to play back all of your pictures in the slideshow.

2. Tap the Slideshow button. The Slideshow Options popover appears (**Figure 5.10**).

3. If you want music to play during the slideshow, set the Play Music switch to On. If not, make sure the option is off and skip the next step.

4. Tap the Music button to choose which music to use. The popover becomes a compact version of the music list in the iPod app, where you can navigate your music library by song title, artist, album, playlist, and other criteria.

note Surprisingly, the Photos app lets you play *only one song* during a slideshow; not a playlist, not an album, just one song. I can't imagine it's anything other than a bug in the initial version of the software that shipped with the iPad, and it may even be fixed by the time you read this.

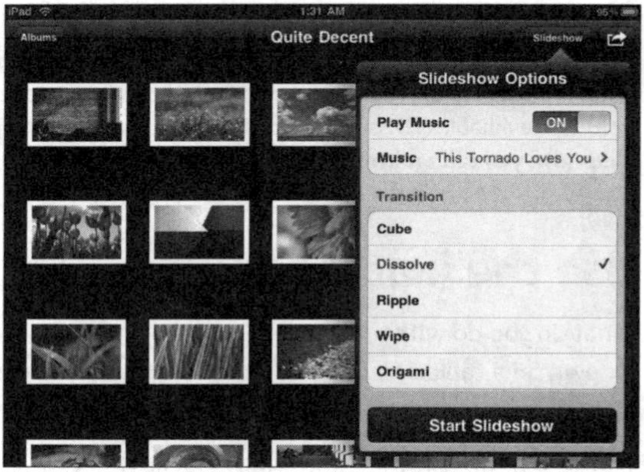

Figure 5.10
Slideshow options

5. Tap a transition style to use.

6. Tap the Start Slideshow button. If you need to cancel the slideshow while it's playing, tap once anywhere on the screen.

The slideshow plays until all photos have been displayed or until the music ends. However, you can customize a few of the slideshow parameters. Go to Settings > Photos, where you can specify how long each slide appears onscreen (in increments from 2 to 20 seconds), whether the photos (and music) repeat after they've initially appeared, and whether the order should be shuffled (**Figure 5.11**). These settings apply to any slideshow you run in the Photos app.

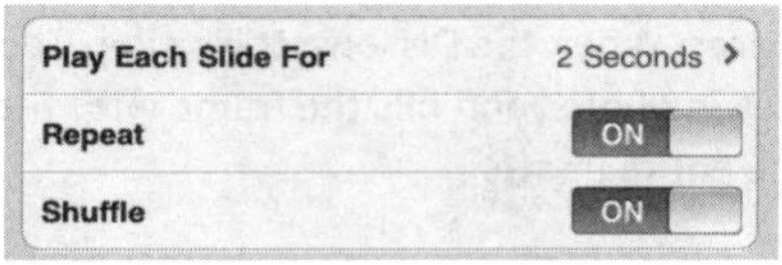

Figure 5.11
Slideshow preferences

tip The Photos app respects the order in which the pictures were sorted before you synced them. If you want a custom order, set it up in your photo software.

tip With the addition of Apple's iPad Dock Connector to VGA Adapter, you can play the slideshow on a projector or monitor. However, the only transition available is Dissolve. Also, the signal is sent only when you're running a slideshow; you can't mirror the iPad's screen on the connected screen.

Use the iPad as a Picture Frame

What do you do with an iPad when you're not using it? Instead of setting it down on a table or a stack of mail, put that big screen to use as a digital picture frame.

To activate the feature, simply press the Picture Frame button on the lock screen (**Figure 5.12**). While remaining locked, the screen switches into a slideshow mode. Tap the screen and then tap the button again to exit the Picture Frame mode.

Figure 5.12
Picture Frame button

Picture Frame

You can change some aspects of how the slideshow is presented. Go to Settings > Picture Frame and adjust the following preferences:

- **Transition:** Choose either Dissolve or Origami.
- **Zoom in on Faces:** When the Dissolve transition is enabled, this option discovers faces in photos and fills the frame with them instead of displaying the entire photo.

- **Shuffle:** Present folders in random order.
- **Source:** Choosing All Photos pulls images from the entire photo library. You can also tap Albums, Faces, or Events (if the latter two are available) and then specify a collection.

Share Photos

On more than one occasion I've shown a photo to someone who then said, "Ooh, can you send that to me?" Why yes, I certainly can, and it's easy to do.

Share via email

To attach a photo to an outgoing message, do the following:

1. Open a photo and tap the Action button ().

2. In the popover that appears, tap Email Photo. A new outgoing mail message appears (**Figure 5.13**).

3 Add a recipient, subject, and optional message text in the appropriate fields.

4. Tap the Send button to dispatch the photo.

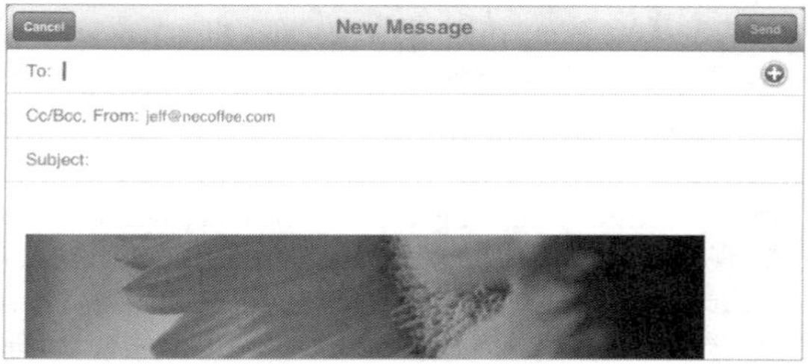

Figure 5.13

Sharing a photo as an email attachment

Share multiple photos via email

It's possible to group several photos into an email message.

1. In the Photos app, tap a collection to open it.

2. Tap the Action button ().

3. Tap the photos you wish to send. Selected ones are marked with a blue checkmark (**Figure 5.14**).

Figure 5.14
Selecting multiple photos for sharing

4. Tap the Email button to create a new outgoing message with the photos as attachments.

5. Address the message and tap the Send button.

tip Many photo sharing services, like Flickr (www.flickr.com), accept uploads via email. You're given a personal Flickr email address, and any image files sent to that address are posted to your photostream.

note Although sending files via email is convenient, I don't recommend ganging up a bunch of images together in one message. That increases the chance that a mail server might think you're sending spam or viruses; or your recipient may not have the bandwidth to deal with such large messages.

Send to MobileMe

Subscribers to Apple's MobileMe service can upload files to an online gallery, where other people can view or download the image.

1. Open a photo and tap the Action button (⬆).

2. In the popover that appears, tap Send to MobileMe.

3. Give the photo a title and description in the Publish Photo dialog (**Figure 5.15**).

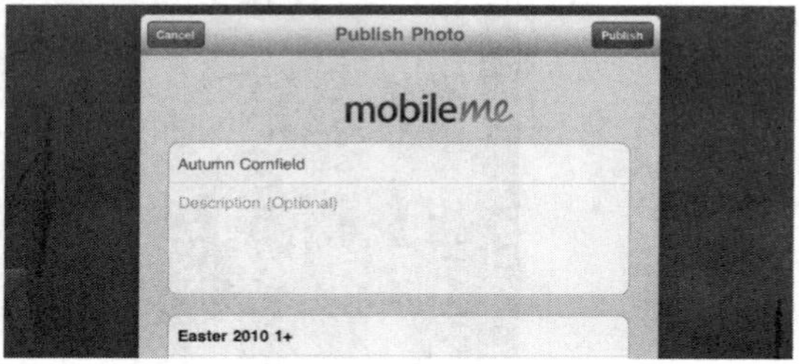

Figure 5.15
Selecting multiple photos for sharing

Cancel	Publish Photo	Publish

mobile*me*

Autumn Cornfield

Description (Optional)

Easter 2010 1+

4. Tap an album name where the photo will appear.

 If you want to create a new album, you'll need to do it either at the me.com site on your computer or in iPhoto or Aperture, not in the Photos app. For now, upload to any album and then move it later.

5. Tap the Publish button.

6. After the file is uploaded, a dialog gives you the option to view the photo in Safari, send an email to a friend with a link to the Web page, or close the dialog.

The capability to select and upload multiple photos isn't supported when publishing to a MobileMe gallery.

Assign to Contact

If you have a photo of a friend whose information is in your Contacts app, choose the Assign to Contact option from the Action popover. Select the person's name in the Contacts list that appears, then pinch and drag to position the photo in the frame (**Figure 5.16**). Tap the Use button to assign the photo.

Figure 5.16
Assigning a photo to a contact

Use as Wallpaper

I covered how to set wallpapers in the iPad's Settings app, but in Photos you can do it directly. Choose Use as Wallpaper from the popover, then choose Set Lock Screen, Set Home Screen, or Set Both (see Chapter 1).

Copy Photo

To copy the image to the iPad's temporary memory, choose Copy Photo from the popover. You can also tap and hold a photo thumbnail when viewing the collection and choose Copy. With the image copied, you can paste it elsewhere, such as in another app or in an outgoing email message.

Sync imported photos and videos back to the computer

You probably don't intend to keep photos you imported using the iPad Camera Connection Kit in the iPad's memory. When you get back to your computer, do the following to move them to its hard drive.

1. Connect the iPad to the computer.

2. Open your photo management software (such as iPhoto or Photoshop Elements for Windows).

3. Use the software's feature for importing photos, just as if you'd attached a camera.

   The computer sees the iPad as a USB storage device. Under Windows, you can view it as you would view an attached disk. On the Mac, you need to use photo software or the Image Capture application to access the iPad's pictures.

4. After importing the files, delete them from the iPad: Open a collection, tap the Action button (), tap to select the images you want to remove, and then tap the Delete button. Tap the Delete Selected Photos button that appears (to confirm your action).

   tip At the beginning of this chapter, I explained that iTunes optimizes photos when syncing them to the iPad. However, images imported using the iPad Camera Connection Kit retain their original size, image quality, and metadata. If it's important to have high-resolution versions on the iPad—for example, if you're using it as a portfolio and you want to email an original Raw file to someone—importing them using the camera adapters is the way to go.

Photo Apps from Other Developers

The Photos app is designed primarily for viewing photos, but other developers are taking advantage of the iPad's graphics capabilities to make interesting photographic apps. Here are a few examples worth looking into; the Photography category at the App Store contains hundreds of iPad-compatible apps.

- **Photogene for iPad:** If you're looking for a "Photoshop for the iPad," this app comes close. Apply presets to a photo, or go manual with luminance and color sliders, curves, filters, and frames.

- **PhotoCalc:** This handy app doesn't do anything with your photos, but if you're a photographer, you'll find it helpful. It provides calculations for determining depth of field settings, flash power output recommendations, and a solar calculator that tells you when sunrise and sunset will occur in your current location.

- **CameraBag for iPad:** This well-designed set of filters mimics popular photo styles, such as Helga (with results that look like old Russian-made inexpensive Holga cameras), Instant, 1962, 1974, and Silver.

- **Flickr, SmugMug, Photobucket, Picasa:** These apps from popular photo sharing sites let you view and upload your photos as well as browse other members' photo collections.

6

Read Books

Under other circumstances, the subject of reading electronic books on a device would warrant a few paragraphs, or maybe an extended sidebar. But the iPad's handheld form factor and large storage capacity makes it an attractive ebook reader. It wouldn't surprise me if some people view the iPad primarily as an ebook reader that also happens to do other stuff.

Instead of packing a tote bag bursting with hardcovers on your next vacation, Apple's iBooks app offers an attractive alternative: store digital versions of books on the iPad, and connect to the iBookstore to buy new ones when you need more.

Note that although this chapter focuses on the features of the iBooks app, that's not the only player out there. If you previously owned an Amazon Kindle e-reader, you can download Amazon's free Kindle app and keep your existing library. (Some people may prefer to use the Kindle software entirely, since currently Amazon offers many more titles than the iBookstore.)

The iPad can also handle other types of electronic text. Many media companies, already buffeted by a shaky economy and a slow start on confronting new technologies, are hoping the iPad will glide in and save them by offering digital versions of magazines and newspapers. That's a lot of weight to put onto a 1.5-pound tablet, and it's still too early to see what difference the iPad (and other tablets) will make. For now, media other than books are viewed in Safari (the companies' Web sites) and in standalone apps, like the Wall Street Journal, New York Times, and Popular Mechanics.

Install the iBooks App

The iBooks app isn't included on the iPad by default. In iTunes or using the App Store on the iPad, search for "iBooks." Download and install the free app.

 note **As of May 2010, iBooks is available only to customers in the United States. As Apple negotiates deals with publishers, I'm hoping iBooks becomes available to international markets soon.**

Browse Your Library

When you open the iBooks app, you see your books arranged on a faux wooden shelf (**Figure 6.1**). Swipe up to reveal more books as your collection grows.

tip **Swipe down as far as you can to reveal a little hidden surprise in the bookshelf.**

Figure 6.1
The iBooks library

Icon or List view

Rearrange or remove books

Normally, books appear in the order you add them to the library, with the most recent title appearing at the top-left location. You can move books around easily: tap the Edit button, touch and hold a title, and drag it to a new spot.

The Edit mode also exposes the Delete button (the X) at the upper-left corner. Just as you would do to remove apps from the Home screen (explained in Chapter 2), tap that button to remove the title from your library.

tip   Books are backed up to your computer when you sync to iTunes. If you want to keep a book on your computer but temporarily remove it from the library, make sure you sync before deleting it.

Although this view is attractive, the endless bookshelf doesn't work as well after you've added many titles. For more detail, tap the List view button (**Figure 6.2**).

Figure 6.2
*Sort options in
the List view*

The List view presents more options for organizing the library. Tap one of
the buttons at the bottom of the screen to re-order the list.

Titles in the Bookshelf list view can be re-ordered, just as they can in
the main Bookshelf view. Tap the Edit button and then drag the icon
that appears at the far right edge of the row.

To delete a book quickly in the List view, swipe its title left-to-right (or
right-to-left), then tap the Delete button that appears.

Search for books

When the number of books in your library starts to get really out of
control (or, as my step-sister would say, "A good start"), you can use the
Search Books field at the top of the List view to locate a title. Start typing
a title or author name to narrow the list (**Figure 6.3**).

Figure 6.3
*Searching
for books*

Read a Book

To get you started, Apple includes a copy of A. A. Milne's *Winnie-the-Pooh* with the iBooks app. To open a book, tap its cover.

The appearance of the book changes based on the iPad's rotation (**Figure 6.4**). When viewed in portrait orientation, you see one page at a time. Turn it to landscape view and the text is split over two pages.

Figure 6.4
iBooks rotation

Portrait orientation

Landscape orientation

tip Use the Rotation Lock switch, located just above the volume controls on the right edge of the iPad, to keep the screen from rotating if you shift and read while lying on your side or otherwise change position.

Navigate the book

It feels a little funny that I should tell you how to read a book (obviously, you're doing a fine job reading my book), but there are a few things to note before you get absorbed by the content you're about to read.

- Tap the middle of the screen to reveal the reading controls if they're not visible. (Tap again to make them disappear.)

- To turn the next page, swipe right to left. Swipe left to right to go to the previous page. You don't need to swipe the width of the page; a small swipe works the same.

  For kicks, drag the page edge slowly (**Figure 6.5**): Apple made a point of reproducing the look of curling the page, complete with a preview of what's on the next page (in landscape mode) or ghosted, reversed letters that would show through typical book-quality paper.

- Tap the right or left edge of the screen to turn the page using a faster, minimal animation.

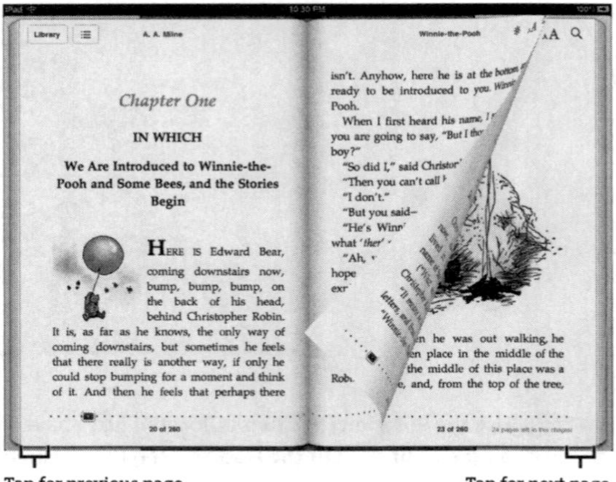

Figure 6.5
Turning pages

Tap for previous page.   Tap for next page.

tip In the iBooks preferences (go to Settings > iBooks) is the option to specify what happens when you tap the left margin. By default it takes you to the previous page, but if you don't anticipate going backwards (you forward-thinking reader, you), tap the Tap Left Margin button and choose Next Page instead of Previous Page. You can still go to the previous page by swiping left-to-right anywhere on the screen.

- Tap the Contents button (≡) to view the table of contents. You can tap a chapter or section to navigate to it, or tap the Resume button (which looks like a red bookmark) to go back to where you were.

- Drag the navigation control at the bottom of the screen to jump to a specific page or chapter (**Figure 6.6**).

Figure 6.6
Advancing to another section of the book

note I love that the lower-right corner tells you how many pages are left in the current chapter. How many times have you been reading in bed, almost at the verge of sleep, but decided to push on until the end of the chapter? In iBooks, you don't have to flip ahead to see how much further ahead the next chapter is.

Search the book's text

Another way to navigate a book is to look for occurrences of specific text (or, I suppose, to find out how many times an author swears throughout the text). The number of matches appears at the bottom of the results list. This feature also provides convenient Search Google and Search Wikipedia buttons to expand your search in Safari.

1. Tap the middle of the screen to display the reading controls.

2. Tap the Search button in the upper-right corner.

3. Type a search term and tap the Search button on the onscreen keyboard, or wait a few seconds for results to appear (**Figure 6.7**).

4. Scroll through the results to find the one you want, and then tap it to go to that place in the book. The term is highlighted to find it easily.

   Or, tap outside the popover to dismiss it.

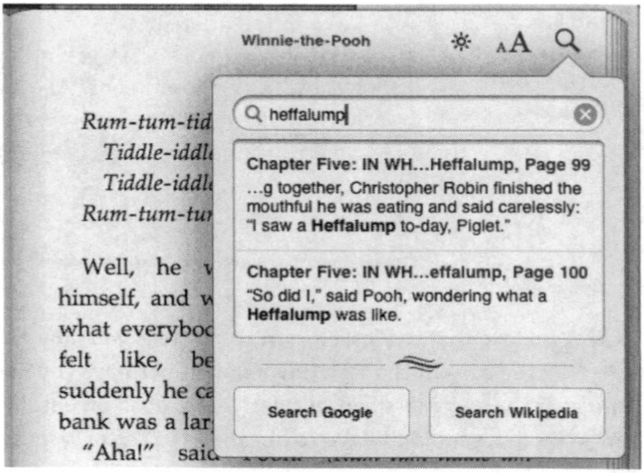

Figure 6.7
Searching the book

When you tap the Search button again, the previous results are still available.

A slightly faster method of searching is available when you select a word or phrase on a page.

1. Touch and hold to select the text you want to find.

2. From the options that appear, tap the Search button (**Figure 6.8**). The search results popover appears.

Figure 6.8
*Searching
by selection*

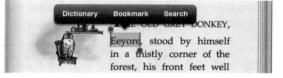

Change the Book's Appearance

Reading is a personal experience, and iBooks offers a few options for customizing the appearance of your books.

Adjust screen brightness

The iPad's bright screen becomes a liability when it's flooding the bedroom with light and preventing your partner from sleeping or when it's intimidating the pets. Tap the Brightness button to expose a slider that changes the brightness level (**Figure 6.9**). This control is far more convenient than adjusting brightness in the Settings app.

Figure 6.9
*The Brightness
slider*

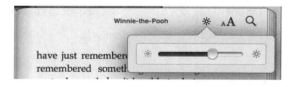

note The Brightness setting in iBooks is applied system-wide, so it sticks when you leave the iBooks app. You can open Settings > Brightness & Wallpaper to bring the backlight level up.

Change text size and font

One noticeable advantage of electronic books is that you can adjust the type size to match what's comfortable for your eyes.

1. Tap the Font button next to the Brightness button to display a popover with text options (**Figure 6.10**).

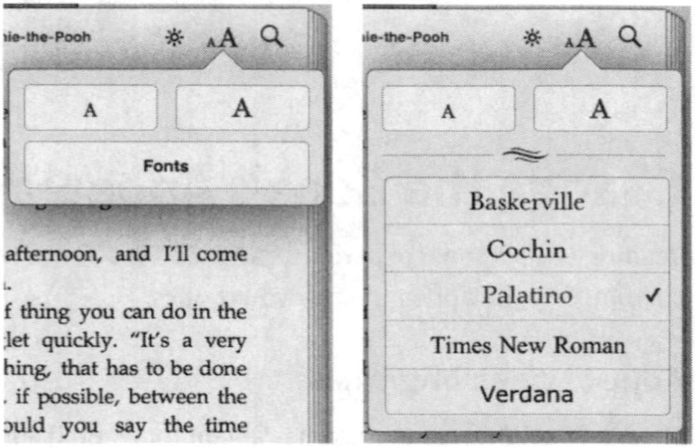

Figure 6.10
Adjusting text size and font

2. Tap the small A button to make the text smaller, or tap the large A button to make it larger.

3. Tap the Fonts button to reveal the typeface options.

4. Tap one of the font names to use that for the book's text.

5. Tap outside the popover to dismiss it.

Set Bookmarks

iBooks doesn't include the ability to make notes in the virtual margins, but you can highlight sections and create a bookmark for coming back later.

Create a new bookmark

1. Select a section of text you want to bookmark.

2. From the options that appear, tap Bookmark. The selection appears as if you'd marked it with a highlighter (**Figure 6.11**).

Figure 6.11
Creating a new bookmark

Bookmarks
(highlighted)

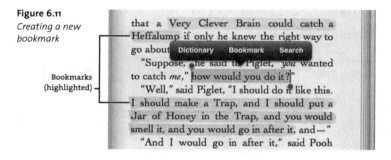

3. Once the bookmark is created, tap it to view options for changing the highlighter color or removing the bookmark (**Figure 6.12**). The next bookmark you create shares the same color.

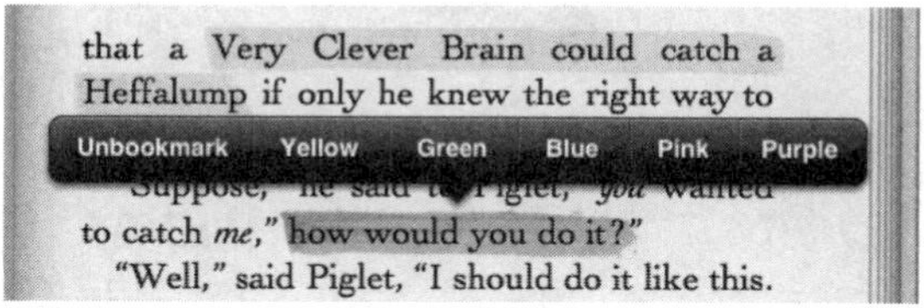

Figure 6.12
Choosing a highlight color

tip I like to categorize things by color, so the bookmark highlight options make me happy. (As does the way the bookmarks look like they're drawn with a real highlighter pen.) I'm sure the point is to simply let you choose your favorite color, but I can imagine two people sharing an iPad using colored bookmarks to read the same book. Or marking up text for different categories in a textbook, for example.

Return to a bookmark

When it's time to go back to something you bookmarked, do the following:

1. Tap the Contents button (≡) to view the table of contents.

2. Tap the Bookmarks button (**Figure 6.13**).

3. Tap a bookmark from the list to go to that page.

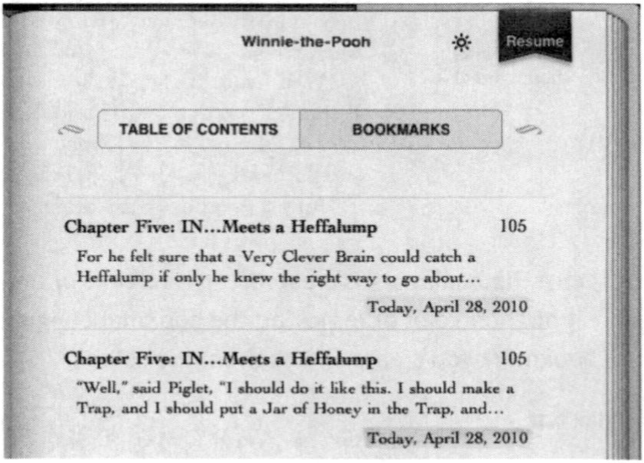

Figure 6.13
Bookmarks list

Look up Word Definitions

One of the great joys (and sometimes great frustrations) of reading is coming across unfamiliar words. iBooks offers a built-in dictionary lookup feature.

1. Touch and hold a word to select it.

2. From the options that appear, tap the Dictionary button. A definition appears (**Figure 6.14**).

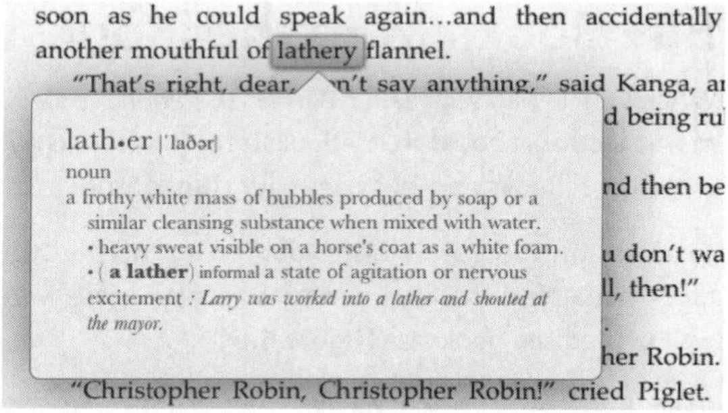

Figure 6.14
Viewing a definition

soon as he could speak again…and then accidentally another mouthful of lathery flannel.

"That's right, dear, n't say anything," said Kanga, and being ru

lath·er |ˈlaðər|
noun
a frothy white mass of bubbles produced by soap or a similar cleansing substance when mixed with water.
• heavy sweat visible on a horse's coat as a white foam.
• (a lather) informal a state of agitation or nervous excitement : *Larry was worked into a lather and shouted at the mayor.*

nd then be

u don't wa

ll, then!"

her Robin.

"Christopher Robin, Christopher Robin!" cried Piglet.

Reading Books Aloud with VoiceOver

The iPad includes VoiceOver, an accessibility feature for people with limited vision that reads aloud text and the names of onscreen elements. I assumed that meant I could have iBooks read a book to me while I'm cooking, driving, or otherwise would want a textbook act like an audiobook.

Unfortunately, that's not the case. With VoiceOver enabled, the iPad can read only one page at a time. It's not onerous, but it's not too convenient, either. I'm sure this is more of a licensing issue than a technological one, since publishers negotiate separate licenses for audio versions of books. For now, ebooks and audio books remain separate entities. If you want to give it a try, do the following:

1. In Settings > General > Accessiblity > VoiceOver, tap the VoiceOver switch to On.

2. In a book within iBooks, tap once anywhere in the text and then double-tap the screen to begin reading the page.

3. To turn to the next page, swipe three fingers right-to-left on the screen; VoiceOver reads that page and stops.

Buy Books from the iBookstore

When you've had your fill of *Winnie-the-Pooh*, Apple is ready to sell you more electronic books in its iBookstore. The store is available only from within the iBooks app, but uses your iTunes Store account.

To access the iBookstore from your library, tap the Store button. In a great bit of visual flair, the library rotates as if the store were a hidden passageway behind the bookcase (**Figure 6.15**).

Figure 6.15
"Put...the... candle...back!"

The library rotates...   ...to reveal the iBookstore.

Browsing the iBookstore is similar to shopping at the iTunes Store:

- Tap a book title to view more information about it (**Figure 6.16**).

- To purchase the book, tap the price button, which changes to read "Buy Book." Tap the button again to buy the book, which, after you enter your account and password, downloads and appears in your library.

- Tap the Get Sample button to download a sample (usually the first chapter or a sizable excerpt. It appears in your library with a Sample banner on the cover (**Figure 6.17**). If you like the book, tap the Buy button that appears at the top of the screen.

tip Tap the Categories button at the top of the iBookstore screen to locate books in various genres. You can also browse the New York Times best-seller list by tapping the NYTimes button in the toolbar, or view Oprah's Book Club titles using a link found when you scroll to the end of the page.

Figure 6.16
Viewing more info about a book

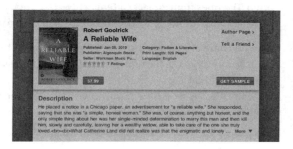

tip You don't have to shell out money to get a taste of iBooks titles. Scroll to the bottom of the iBookstore page and tap the Free Books link to view plenty of books from Project Gutenberg.

Figure 6.17
A sample of a book

Sample banner   Buy title from within the sample.

note Books purchased from the iBookstore are protected by Apple's FairPlay digital rights management (DRM) scheme, which means you can't give the book to someone else when you're finished reading, as you can with a print book. That also adds an unfortunate (and stupid) limitation: you can't copy any selected text in a book purchased from the store.

Import Your Own Ebooks

Books from the iBookstore are formatted as EPUB files, an open format designed for electronic publishing by the International Digital Publishing Forum. The titles from Project Gutenberg (www.gutenberg.org) are all EPUB files, without Apple's DRM, and are available from other sources.

If you purchase or download an EPUB file, you can add the book to your iBooks library. Drag the file to the Library section in the sidebar, or to the iTunes application icon; you can also choose File > Add to Library and locate the file. The next time you sync with the iPad, the book is added to your library.

Creating Your Own EPUB Books

Writing a novel? Or perhaps you have an electronic book formatted as a PDF or text-only file. With the assistance of a few utilities, you can build your own EPUB files for viewing in iBooks (or any other reader that accepts the format). Here are a few examples:

- Calibre (calibre-ebook.com) is an application available for Windows, Mac OS X, and Linux that accepts several text formats and converts a document to an ePub.

- Storyist (storyist.com) for Mac OS X includes support for outputting EPUB files, including adding images.

- Adobe InDesign (adobe.com) is the big gorilla in this zoo, with support for creating Adobe Digital Editions as EPUB files.

- Stanza Desktop (www.lexcycle.com) was designed to create EPUB files for the Stanza iPhone app, but the files also work in iBooks. (Stanza was my favorite e-reader on the iPhone, but the company was purchased by Amazon, so I doubt an iPad version will appear.)

note Before you purchase EPUB books online, make sure you know what you're buying. Not every EPUB file will work with the iPad. Titles from Kobo (www.kobobooks.com), for example, are EPUB formatted, but are protected by Adobe DRM. (You can download the free eBooks by Kobo HD app to read them, but then you're adding another e-reader to your collection.)

Other Ebook Readers

iBooks is the Apple-designed option, but of course there are other applications out there (such as a little Amazon.com offering you may have heard of). In fact, one of the most interesting developments in electronic books isn't happening within e-readers at all—publishers are writing iPad *apps*, not just files, that do so much more than turn pages.

Kindle for iPad

When people think of Amazon's Kindle, they picture the hardware: slim devices with grayscale E-Ink screens that store lots of ebooks and have great battery life. What they often forget is that Amazon offers Kindle for iPad, an app that brings the reading experience to the iPad. The app offers a cleaner look than iBooks—it's not trying to replicate physical books and pages (although page turns do curl like paper). The Kindle for iPad app also currently offers three features you won't find in iBooks:

View a book on several devices

Currently the only way to read an iBooks title is on the iPad, though an iPhone version of iBooks is promised with the iPhone OS 4 update coming in summer 2010. Amazon, by contrast, offers Kindle software not only for the Kindle devices and iPad, but for the iPhone, Windows, Mac OS X, and Blackberry devices. When you read a book in one location, your place is marked in other clients, too.

Larger catalog

Amazon had a two-year head start on Apple in the ebook field, so the Kindle offerings are much broader than the iBookstore (Amazon claims 500,000 titles, while Apple says it has "tens of thousands" of books). For a while at least, if you can't find a book at the iBookstore, it's likely you can buy it from Amazon.

Mark up text with inline notes

1. Tap the screen to display the reading controls.

2. Touch and hold a word where you want to add a note.

3. Type a note in the field that appears, and then tap Save (**Figure 6.18**). A small note icon appears next to the word; tapping it reveals the text as a balloon.

   More important, the note is synchronized with all copies of that book on other devices.

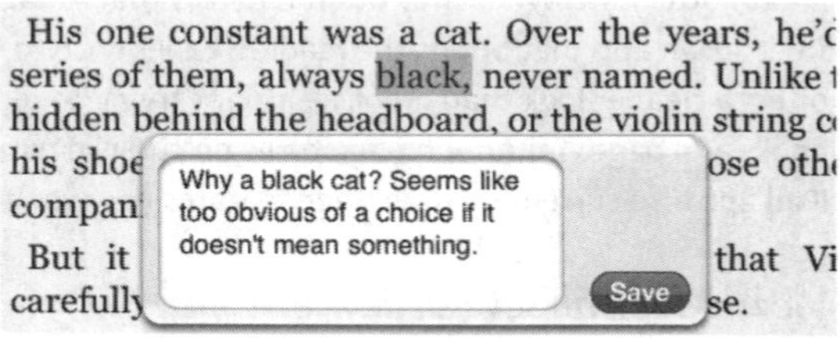

Figure 6.18
Adding a note in Kindle for iPad

His one constant was a cat. Over the years, he'c series of them, always black, never named. Unlike t hidden behind the headboard, or the violin string c his shoe   ose oth
compan: Why a black cat? Seems like
          too obvious of a choice if it
   But it doesn't mean something.   that Vi
carefull   Save   se.

tip It's not obvious how to remove a note in the Kindle app. Tap the note icon to display the text, then touch and hold the note for a second. You're then asked if you want to delete the note, which will be removed on all editions of the file.

Standalone apps

iBooks and the Kindle app are great for reading books that are mostly text, like novels or non-fiction narratives. But remember, the iPad is a computer with impressive processor and graphics performance. As a result, publishers also offer standalone apps for books that include not only the core text, but other multimedia content.

For example, many children's books have options to read the story aloud, play games, and color on the screen (**Figure 6.19**). Reference works, such as *The Elements: A Visual Exploration*, can convey much more information than the facts and some photos.

Figure 6.19
Coloring in the Miss Spider app

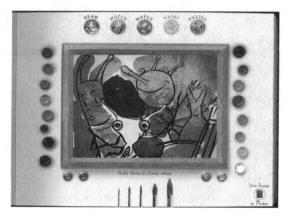

Comic Books

Since its release, I can't tell you how many reviewers (myself included) have pointed out that the iPad could be the enticement that makes them start reading comics again. Apps like Marvel, iVerse, and IDW provide the framework for reading (**Figure 6.20**) and then let you purchase issues within the app.

Figure 6.20
The Marvel Comics app

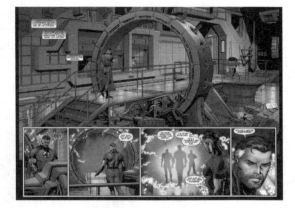

Read Other Text

I can't wrap up this chapter without talking about a couple of other text circumstances that don't fall neatly into the "books" category.

Instapaper

By far my favorite app on the iPad so far, Instapaper takes articles on Web pages and saves them for reading later.

Several times a day I run across longform pieces of text that I want to read, but if I read them all right away I can't get any work done. So I use a bookmarklet to send the pages to Instapaper.com (see Chapter 3 for more on bookmarklets). Later, I can launch the Instapaper app on my iPad, which syncs its content with instapaper.com, and pick which ones I want to read (**Figure 6.21**).

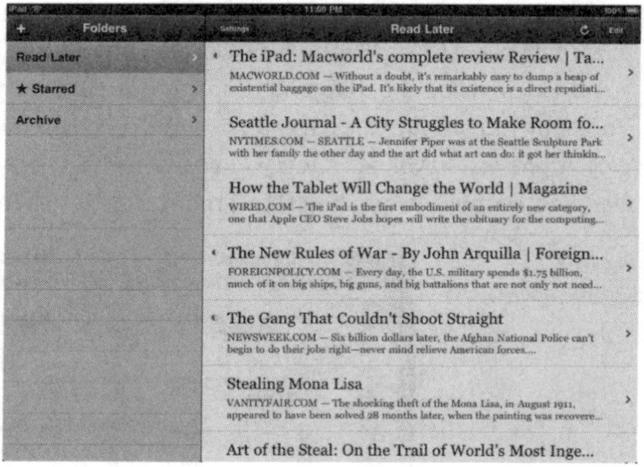

Figure 6.21
Articles waiting to be read in Instapaper

Not only is it easy to find the articles I want to read later, Instapaper formats them using clean typography and without the ads and other cruft that surroundsc most content on the Web.

Read PDF files with GoodReader

In Chapter 4, I discussed handling file attachments in the Mail app, one main method of getting files onto the iPad. The operating system can open many file types, including PDF and Microsoft Word files, that you're likely to encounter.

The problem is that you're just getting a look at those files without much other control. With PDFs especially, that can be frustrating, because internal links don't work, you can't jump to a page much further into a long document, and more.

To overcome those limitations, download the PDF viewer to end them all: GoodReader (www.goodiware.com).

GoodReader is one of those apps that does so much you feel like you're scratching the surface (**Figure 6.22**). You can import files (PDF, Office, iWork, audio, video) using the drag-and-drop interface in the Apps pane within iTunes, by transferring files over a Wi-Fi network, or downloading from the Web. It preserves Web links, lets you add bookmarks, password-protect files, and, so much more than I have room to go into here.

Figure 6.22
GoodReader

7

Entertain Yourself

Laptops took computing off the desk and made it more portable, but using one for enjoyable pursuits like watching movies always feels a bit like work, as if you're going to the theater and being seated in a cubicle. The keyboard is in the way, and with most laptops you find yourself scrambling to find and plug in the power cord right as something exciting is happening in the movie.

On the iPad, the movie is right there on the screen. Your music library is a few taps away. YouTube movies are ready to be streamed. As I discuss elsewhere in the book, the iPad can be incredibly productive, but it can also be a lot of fun.

Sync Media

It is odd that we use i*Tunes* as the central hub for syncing all information to the iPad, but during the early years of the iPod the only data to sync were music files. Since then, our music and movie libraries have grown alongside the capacities of Apple's players, using iTunes as the storehouse for most of our digital entertainment. I've already covered the basics of syncing in Chapter 1, so in this section I'll highlight sync options that pertain specifically to music, videos, audiobooks, and podcasts.

Choose which media to sync

Depending upon the size of your iTunes media library, you may have no trouble synchronizing everything to the iPad (which is the default setting). But even if there is room, you may want to be more choosy about how you fill those bytes (so you're not stumbling over your collection of kids' music while on a business trip, for example).

1. Connect the iPad to your computer and select it in the sidebar within iTunes.

2. Click the Music tab.

3. Ensure that the Sync Music checkbox is enabled, and then choose the radio button for Selected playlists, artists, and genres (**Figure 7.1**).

4. Choose any of the following options (or ignore them and go to the next step):

   ■ **Include music videos:** You can purchase music videos from the iTunes Store, and some albums include videos as bonus material. With this box checked, the videos are copied along with the music. However, the iPad doesn't quite know how to deal with them, surprisingly. If a video comes up when listening to an album, just the music plays. If you tap a music video in the iPad app (which could be by accident, as there's no indication that the track is a video), you get to see the video. However, as soon as it's done, you'll discover you've been handed off to the Videos app, and therefore the next song in your iPod list won't play. Also, you can play only one video at a time, even in the Videos app. (Didn't anyone at Apple ever watch MTV?)

- **Include voice memos:** This option is a holdover from the iPhone, which includes a Voice Memos application.

- **Automatically fill space with songs:** You bought a 32 GB iPad and don't want to waste any of that free space? This option packs the memory full of music beyond what you specify in the fields below.

Figure 7.1
*Syncing Music
in iTunes*

5. In the Playlists, Artists, and Genres lists, click checkboxes belonging to any items you wish to transfer to the iPad. Use the Search field above the Artists list to find artists quickly.

6. Click the Apply button to sync with the new options.

tip Two general sync settings that appear on the iPad summary pane in iTunes let you fit more media onto the device. "Convert higher bit rate songs to 128 kbps AAC" downsamples audio to a lower quality, reducing the songs' files sizes. "Prefer standard definition videos" leaves larger-sized HD movies on your computer and transfers only standard definition ones.

note The "Manually manage music and videos" option lets you drag songs and video from your library to the iPad in the sidebar, which would be fine if your media library isn't too large. But these days, I'd rather specify playlists than micro-manage every file.

Create a smart playlist in iTunes

The best thing you can do for the iPod app is create smart playlists in iTunes. A normal playlist contains a fixed set of songs that you add manually. A smart playlist generates its content based on criteria you specify. For example, I sync a smart playlist that includes any media that's been added to iTunes within the last month. Here's how to build it:

1. In iTunes, choose File > New Smart Playlist.

2. Give the playlist a name.

3. From the pop-up menu, choose a selector and conditions (**Figure 7.2**).

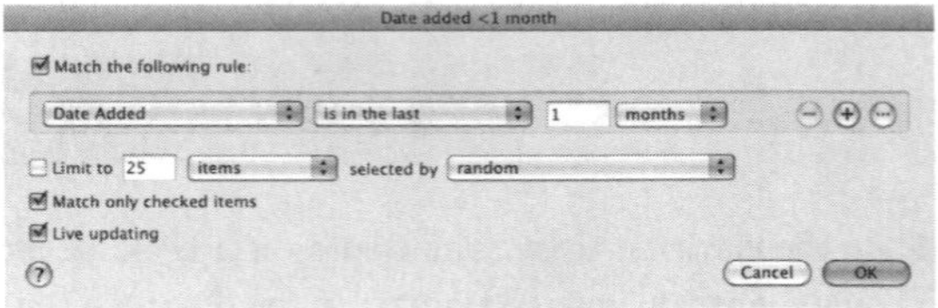

Figure 7.2
Creating a Smart Playlist in Tunes

4. Add more selectors to determine which results appear.

5. Click OK to save the smart playlist.

The next time you set up your sync criteria when the iPad is connected, choose that playlist. Each time you sync, the playlist is updated with new songs.

Play Music

If you're familiar with iTunes, you'll have no trouble playing music in the iPod app. That said, the iPod interface has a few peculiarities.

1. Tap a button at the bottom of the screen to view your library by song, artist, album, genre, or composer (**Figure 7.3**).

Figure 7.3
The iPod interface

Library view options

2. Tap the name of a song to start playing it. The listing determines how you get to that point:

   - **Songs:** The song list is arranged alphabetically, so the songs will play back in that order.

   - **Artists:** Tap an artist's name to view songs, arranged according to the albums on which they appear. If more than one album is listed,

playback stops at the end of an album; you can get around this by
tapping the Play All Songs button at the top of the list.

- **Albums:** Tap an album cover to view its songs, then tap a song
  to start playing. Albums are listed alphabetically by album title
  (**Figure 7.4**).

Figure 7.4
*A track list in the
Albums view*

- **Genres:** Tap the icon for a genre to view albums and songs of that
  musical style. The songs are grouped by album, but playback does
  not stop at the end of the album.

- **Composers:** Tap the name of a composer to view songs he or she
  has composed, then tap a song to begin playing. When multiple
  albums appear, playback ends when the album does.

3. The first song you play displays the Now Playing screen, which
   presents the song's album art, full screen; tap once anywhere to
   reveal its controls (**Figure 7.5**).

   In addition to offering controls for music playback and volume, the
   Now Playing screen includes a button to view the tracks belonging
   to the song's album; you can also double-tap the screen. To return to
   the library view (without stopping playback), tap the button in the
   lower left corner of the screen.

Figure 7.5
*Now Playing
screen*

Return to library view   View album tracks

To return to the Now Playing screen at any time, tap the album art at the lower-left corner of the library screen.

tip   The Now Playing screen is the only location where you can rate a song. Double-tap the screen to reveal album tracks and then, just above the track list, tap a rating (from one to five stars) for the currently playing track.

Navigate songs

While you're listening to audio, use the following controls to skip tracks, rewind, or fast-forward through a song (**Figure 7.6**).

Figure 7.6
Playback controls

Previous   Play/Pause   Next   Playhead

3:32   -0:49

- Tap the Play/Pause button to start or stop playback.

- Tap the Previous button once to return to the beginning of the current song. Tap it twice to play the previous song in the list.

- Tap the Next button once to skip to the next song.

- Touch and hold the Previous or Next button to rewind or fast-forward through a track; holding the button longer speeds up playback.

- Touch and drag the playhead to "scrub" to another section of a track.

tip For more control when scrubbing in the Now Playing screen, touch and hold the playhead and then drag your finger *down*. You'll see the scrubbing speed appear beneath the bar (Figure 7.7). The farther down you drag, the more control you have when you then drag left or right. This feature is especially useful when moving through podcasts, audiobooks, or other lengthy tracks.

tip While music is playing, but the iPad's screen is locked or you're in a different app, press the Home button twice to bring up a small set of playback controls. (You can disable this feature in Settings > General > Home.)

Figure 7.7
Scrubbing

Scrubbing speed —

Shuffle songs

To introduce some randomness into your music listening, set your library to shuffle mode. While playing any song, enter the Now Playing screen and tap the shuffle button ( ).

tip Since Apple effectively obscured this feature, I think the following qualifies as a tip: When you're in the Songs view, swipe down to reveal a Shuffle button at the top of the list. Normally the command is hidden under the playback controls.

> **tip** If you own an iPhone or iPod touch, you're probably familiar with the shake-to-shuffle feature: simply shake the device, and the accellerometer recognizes the action and switches to shuffle play mode. The iPod app on the iPad doesn't support that feature—believe me, I tried shaking, twisting, and waving my iPad and only got strange looks from the other people on the bus. It's possible shake-to-shuffle just didn't make it into the initial feature set, but my guess is that the iPad is just large enough that shaking isn't as practical when listening to music.

Repeat playback

Do you have a favorite album that begs to be repeated? In the Now Playing screen, tap the repeat button (⟳) once to replay an album. Tap it again to replay the current song.

Play Genius Mixes

iTunes includes a feature called Genius Mixes, which assemble playlists based on the contents of your music library. Genius Mixes show up as albums when you sync, and are accessible from the Genius Mixes sidebar item in the iPod app. Tap a mix to start playing it. Unlike when playing other albums, you can't see (or edit) which songs are included in a Genius Mix—you just have to trust the algorithms (which often do a pretty good job, I must say).

Listen to podcasts and audiobooks

Podcasts and audiobooks use the same playback controls as other audio tracks, but they gain a couple of extra features.

■ **Change reading speed:** Since most podcasts and audiobooks are spoken-word performances, your ears are more sympathetic to changes in playback speed. In the Now Playing screen, tap the speed indicator to the right of the scrubber bar (1x) to switch between 1x (normal), 2x (twice as fast), or ½x (half of normal).

- **Email link:** Tap the email icon to the left of the scrubber bar (⊠) to create a new outgoing message containing a link to the podcast.

- **Rewind 30 seconds:** Did you miss what someone said? Tap the ⟲ button to move the playhead back 30 seconds.

Create Music Playlists

So far we've been dealing with whatever gets sent over from the computer during a sync operation. The iPod app is not an old-style iPod, however. You can build your own playlists, which get synced back the next time you connect.

Build a playlist

For a handpicked playlist, do the following:

1. Tap the New Playlist button in the lower-left corner of the screen (**Figure 7.8**).

Figure 7.8
Playlist buttons

New Playlist ——+
New Genius Playlist

2. Enter a name for the playlist in the dialog that appears, and tap Save.

3. Tap the ⊕ button to add a song to the playlist. The track title becomes gray to indicate it has been included. You can also tap the Sources button to choose which iPod content to build from (**Figure 7.9**).

Figure 7.9
Building a playlist

> **tip** When viewing an album, swipe down to reveal a hidden Add All Songs option.

4. Tap Done to save the playlist, which appears in the sidebar.

5. Reorder or remove the tracks if you wish, then tap the Done button to finish.

> **note** Tap the Edit button that appears at the top of a playlist's track listing if you want to add, delete, or rearrange songs.

Create a Genius playlist

That was quite a lot of work—what if the iPod app could build a custom playlist for you? When you're listening to any song, tap the Genius button (⬛). A set of songs based on the first one appears in the Genius category (**Figure 7.10**). If no song is playing, you're prompted to select a song in your library to use as the basis of the Genius playlist.

Figure 7.10
A Genius playlist

Tap the Refresh button to generate a new list based on the original criteria. If you enjoyed the list, tap the Save button to create a new, regular playlist.

Play Videos

I love movies, but I don't get out to see them often enough. And while there are a few flicks I'd prefer to see with a large group of people, I'm happy to catch up on my movie watching at home on my own time. The iPad is a great for watching a movie (or TV show, or video podcast, or movie you created) when it's most convenient.

Video sync options

Syncing video works the same as syncing music, outlined earlier in the chapter, with one helpful difference. iTunes can automatically sync items that match timely criteria, such as the five most recent unwatched movies, or the 3 least-watched items. This option applies to any video content: movies, TV shows, and podcasts (including audio podcasts, since they're also timely items).

1. Connect the iPad and then, in iTunes, go to the Movies tab.

2. Click the checkbox for Automatically include, and choose a range of items to copy to the iPad (**Figure 7.11**). (Of course, you can also choose not to include any movies automatically.)

3. In the Movies area that lists all available videos, click the checkbox for any item you want copied in addition to the automatic options.

   You can also choose movies that appear in iTunes playlists. Mark any of the items in the Include Movies from Playlists area.

4. Click the Apply button to sync the iPad and copy the movies.

Figure 7.11
Movies sync options

Movie added manually

Watch a movie

Your video content is available in the Videos app on the iPad, with different categories split among panes (such as Rentals, Movies, TV Shows, Podcasts) (**Figure 7.12**).

Figure 7.12
Available movies

note Apple splits music and videos into separate apps on the iPad (iPod and Videos, respectively), but sometimes you'll encounter crossover. For example, I have a Smart Playlist in iTunes that shows anything added within the last two weeks, and when viewing that playlist in the iPod app, I see video podcasts and recent movie additions, too. Tapping the item takes me to the Videos app, however.

1. Tap a video's icon to view more information about it.

2. To begin playing the movie, tap the Play button (**Figure 7.13**). Depending on the content, you can optionally tap the Chapters button to jump ahead to specific sections.

Figure 7.13
Movie info

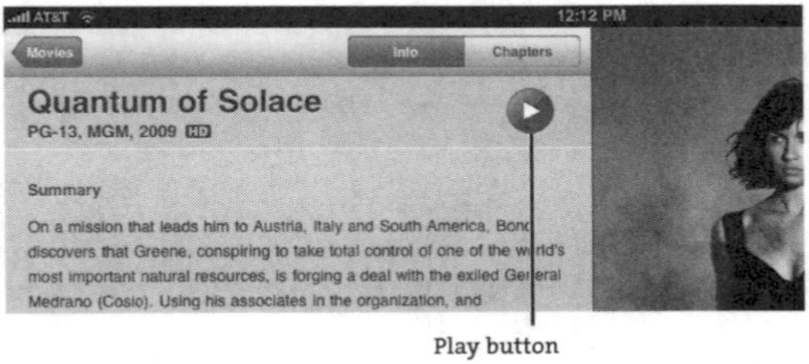

Play button

3. Sit back and enjoy the movie. If you need to interact with playback, tap the screen once to make the onscreen controls appear (**Figure 7.14**):

   - Use the playback controls to play, pause, rewind, or fast-forward. They operate similar to the music controls explained earlier, though tapping once on the Rewind or Fast-forward buttons in long movies skips the video in 5-minute increments.

   - Drag the volume slider to increase or decrease the sound, or use the volume buttons on the iPad case.

   - Drag the playhead to scrub through the movie.

Figure 7.14
Video controls

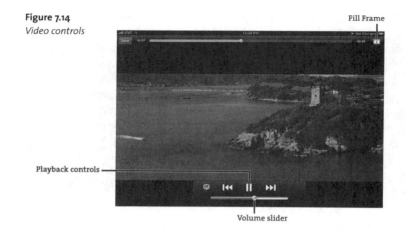

Fill Frame

Playback controls

Volume slider

- When watching widescreen movies, tap the Fill Frame button to use the entire screen (at the expense of cutting off the left and right edges of the picture).

- Some movies also include language or subtitle options, which are accessed by tapping the 🔲 button within the playback controls.

- Tap Done to return to the movie info screen.

Buy or Rent a Movie

You won't be surprised to learn that Apple will happily sell or rent movies to help you fill your time (and your iPad's memory). Go to the iTunes Store in iTunes on your computer, or tap the iTunes app on your iPad. Searching and purchasing movies is similar to buying other things from the iTunes storefronts, but with a few annoying restrictions.

- The iPad can play HD movies, but some titles can only be purchased in SD (standard definition), some can be rented or purchased in SD, and some can be rented in HD only on the iPad. This crazy and confusing distinction is the result of the movies' rights holders (Hollywood studios) trying to wring profit, establish some measure of misguided control, or...well, to be honest I don't know. What's worse is that the availability of these options changes over time; some movies previously available for rent can only be purchased, or no longer appear in the iTunes Store. What this means for you and I is that we need to make sure we examine what we're about to purchase or rent.

- HD movies you rented on the iPad can be viewed only on the iPad, not transferred to your computer or another device.

- After renting a movie, you must watch it within 30 days. If not, the movie is automatically deleted from your library.

- Once you begin to watch a rental, you must finish watching it within 24 hours, at which point it's deleted.

note I apologize for sounding cranky, but I should be able to purchase a movie—in SD or HD, if available—and watch it wherever I want, especially if it's within Apple's ecosystem: buy it on my iPad, watch some of it, then finish watching the movie on my Apple TV or computer. As it is, Apple and the studios are making it difficult for people like me to give them money that I'm willing to part with in exchange for entertainment, which is a terrible business model.

Watch Your Own Movies

The iTunes Store isn't the only source of movies, of course. Home movies you shoot and edit can be viewed on the iPad, too. Export them from your video editing software (such as iMovie or Windows Live Movie Maker) to iTunes as .m4v, .mp4, or .mov formats. Once in iTunes, movies can be synced to the iPad.

Play Videos on a Television

Using a set of Apple cables, you can turn your iPad into something close to a portable version of an Apple TV. There are three options, depending on the type of connection available on the television: the Component AV Cable kit, the Composite AV Cable kit, and the iPad Dock Connector to VGA Adapter. The component kit has the advantage of being digital, versus analog, because it enables you to play protected content (such as videos bought from the iTunes Store).

Although the iPad can play back 720p HD video, you can't watch the same quality through the connection kits. According to the iPad technical specifications, the component kit offers 576p (usually 720 by 576 pixels) and 480p (usually 640 x 480); the composite kit handles 576i and 480i (the same resolutions, but interlaced instead of progressive-scan).

tip My book *iMovie '09 & iDVD: Visual QuickStart Guide* covers all aspects of editing video with iMovie '09, the most recent version as of the release of the iPad. Although it doesn't specifically address exporting to the iPad (I couldn't have predicted the specs a year before the iPad was released), I do talk about how to share movies for the Apple TV. In my testing, I've found that the Apple TV settings work well for the iPad. (In fact, the iPad's video specs are slightly better than the Apple TV, offering 720p HD video at 30 frames per second, while the Apple TV can handle only 24 fps.)

Convert DVDs

What about movies you already own on DVD? Using software such as HandBrake (www.handbrake.fr), you can convert a movie to a digital file that can be imported into iTunes and synced to the iPad. This option is great if you're going on a long trip and don't want to bring along a stack of plastic discs, or for storing kids' entertainment when you don't want the original disc to be damaged. (The iPad, I predict, is going to become a favorite for kids and parents on lengthy car or plane trips.)

note It's worth pointing out here that I'm not a lawyer, and that the practice of encoding DVDs is technically against the law in the United States due to the Digital Millennium Copyright Act (DMCA). Making digital copies of movies you've legally purchased seems like a legitimate fair use to me, and is far preferable to downloading questionably-ripped movies from the Internet. The Electronic Frontier Foundation provides more information about the topic (www.eff.org/IP/digitalvideo/).

Stream Video to the iPad

The iPad is a wireless device, yet you need to connect it to a computer to sync movies and other entertainment to it over the USB cable. Or do you? A few wireless options truly let you watch video almost anywhere.

Streaming video services

Members of the movie rental service Netflix can download the free Netflix app for the iPad and take advantage of the company's growing library of Watch Now titles. The video quality is good, and can even be streamed over a 3G connection. However, be warned that streaming video is bandwidth-intensive. I used up my entire 250 MB data limit watching roughly half of one movie—you'd definitely want the unlimited data option if you plan to watch movies over 3G (see Chapter 1 for information about 3G cellular data plans).

Another popular option is the ABC Player app, which provides streaming versions of entire episodes of ABC's television offerings. (ABC does not allow streaming over a 3G connection, however.) Episodes are typically available the day after they air on broadcast television.

Other services, such as the popular site Hulu.com, have announced plans to release iPad apps that stream their content.

Stream from another computer on your network

Over the years I've accumulated movies and TV shows that now reside on a large hard drive attached to a computer at home. Using programs such as AirVideo (**Figure 7.15**) and StreamToMe, I can watch any of that content while I'm at home. This essentially replicates the functionality of the Apple TV, which can stream video from another computer on the network.

Figure 7.15
AirVideo playing a movie over the network

8

Find Yourself
with Maps

If there's anything about the iPad that makes me feel like I'm living in the future (well, there are a lot of things), it's the Maps app. Within a few seconds, I can look up an address, find a nearby business, go virtual sight-seeing with my daughter, or get directions from my current location—wherever that happens to be—to any address.

The Maps app uses Google's mapping technology to deliver results that can be a typical street map or a top-down satellite view that really does feel like science fiction. As long as you have an Internet connection, you can find yourself. As someone who's never had a good sense of direction, that's incredible.

The iPad Wi-Fi + 3G model includes a GPS chip for accurate location discovery, but the Wi-Fi–only model can also use the feature well.

Find Yourself

For a quick taste of what the Maps app can do, launch it and tap the Current Location () button. The first time you do this, Maps asks for your permission to use your location (**Figure 8.1**).

Figure 8.1
*Allowing Maps
to find you*

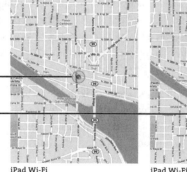

The map zooms in, indicating your location with a blue sphere (**Figure 8.2**). The pale circle emanating from the sphere represents how accurate the location is: a large circle means you're located somewhere within that area. If you see no circle (other than a faint pulse to make the sphere more visible), it means the iPad has pinpointed your location.

Figure 8.2
*Finding location,
Wi-Fi versus GPS*

Location is somewhere within range of this circle.——

Neato movie-style—— visual pulsing effect marking exact location.

iPad Wi-Fi   iPad Wi-Fi + 3G (with GPS)

Location Services: How the iPad Knows Position

The iPad with 3G includes a chip that picks up GPS (Global Positioning Satellite) signals and translates them into an accurate physical location. The Wi-Fi–only model does not contain a GPS chip, but Maps still works. How?

Apple designed a system it calls Location Services, which takes GPS and 3G cellular location data (if available) as well as information from Skyhook Wireless, a company that plots the physical locations of millions of Wi-Fi networks, to come up with an accurate fix on your position. Any app can use Location Services, but it must first ask your permission to use the information. The iPad's operating system keeps track of which apps can access the location data.

It's possible to reset the list (in case you accidentally tapped Don't Allow for an app), although it clears all permissions; you'll need to grant access to apps again the next time they ask. Go to Settings > General > Reset, and tap the Reset Location Warnings button.

You can also just disable Location Services in Settings > General (turn the option to Off). However, some features, such as Find My iPad, will no longer work. You may choose to disable Location Services temporarily, for example, when you want to conserve battery life.

To navigate the map, do any of the following:

- Drag with one finger to reposition the map. As you move around, the map redraws areas previously outside the borders of the frame. At any time you can tap the Current Location button to re-center the map on your position.

- Pinch two fingers to zoom in or out. You can pinch and move at the same time, too.

- Double-tap anywhere on the screen to zoom in on that area.

- Both iPad models include a compass, a chip that can determine which direction it's pointed. Tap the Current Location button again to orient the view according to the direction you're facing (**Figure 8.3**).

Figure 8.3
Compass view

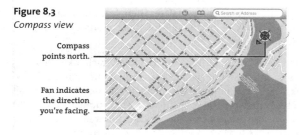

Compass
points north.

Fan indicates
the direction
you're facing.

tip The compass works best when the iPad is held flat, parallel to the ground. You may need to recalibrate it occasionally by (I'm not kidding) waving the iPad in a figure-eight motion in the air.

Map views

The Maps app offers four map views that cater to people who find routes in different ways. If you feel turned around using the Classic style, you may find it helpful to see landmarks in the Satellite view, for instance. To access the other styles, tap the page curl at the lower-right corner of the screen (**Figure 8.4**). Tap a style to switch to it (**Figure 8.5**).

Figure 8.4
Tapping the page curl to reveal Maps settings

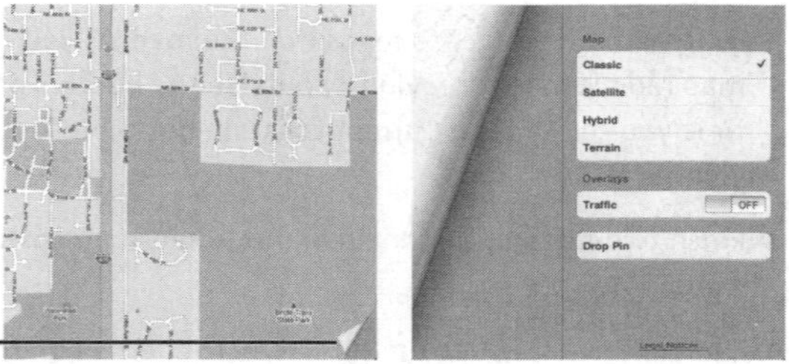

Page curl

tip It's easiest to tap the page curl to view the Maps settings, but for a more leisurely experience, touch and drag the paper's edge. Why? Because you can, of course!

Figure 8.5
A composite of the map styles

Classic   Terrain

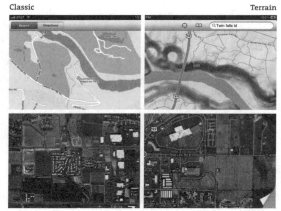

Satellite   Hybrid

Find Locations

Now that you know where you are, it's time to go exploring. The Search field can accept nearly any query, not just addresses. Type "coffee," for example, and results appear as red pins on the map. You can also start typing a specific company name, the name of a person or company in your Contacts list, or the name of an earlier search result.

Tap a pin to identify the location (**Figure 8.6**, on the next page). If you don't see what you're looking for, the match may be outside the current screen view. Tap the 🔘 button in the Search field to display a popover containing all the results.

Figure 8.6
*Search results
as pins*

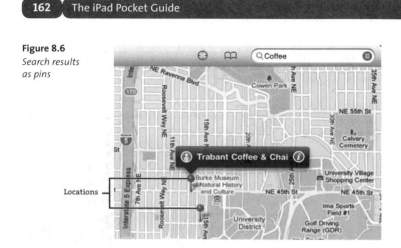

Locations

Get information about a location

To learn more about a location, tap the ⓘ button. The label expands to
display more information and options (**Figure 8.7**).

Figure 8.7
*More information
about a location*

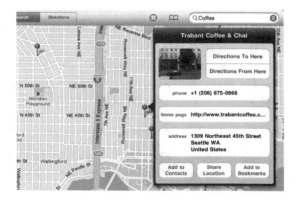

- Tap the Home Page label to visit the site in Safari.

- Tap the Add to Contacts button to create a new contact record containing all of the information.

- Tap the Share Location button to compose an email message containing a URL to view the location on Google Maps and the location as a vCard file (for easy import into most address book applications).

- Tap Add to Bookmarks to save the location for the future. It will be available by tapping the Bookmarks button in the toolbar.

- Tap one of the Directions buttons to view a route to the location; see "Get Directions," coming up in this chapter.

- Touch and hold any field, and then tap the Copy option that appears to copy just that information for pasting elsewhere (such as in an outgoing email message).

Visit the Street View

If you see a Street View icon ( ) on a location's label, tap it to see what the place looks like if you're standing in front of it. I like this feature a lot, because I can better see what a building looks like so I don't miss it (**Figure 8.8**).

Figure 8.8
Street View

Intended location

Tap to navigate
down the street.

Tap to exit
Street View

tip Double-tap or pinch within the Street View mode to zoom in. Tap once again to view the address larger at the top of the screen, as well as a Report button that can be used to report inappropriate content captured by the Street View cameras.

note Consider Street View images as a rough reference, because often something will change—a building repainted, a tree removed—in the time since the photo was taken.

Drop a pin

In addition to finding locations through a search, you can drop a pin on an arbitrary location to get a little more information about it, or to mark a spot for reference.

1. Touch and hold an area of the screen. A purple pin lands there, with the address of the location listed in its label. (**Figure 8.9**).

Figure 8.9
Dropped pin

2. Touch and hold the pin to lift it from the map, and then drag it to a more specific location if you want.

   Tapping the ⓘ icon reveals the options for copying and saving the address. If Street View is available for that location, tap the Street View button to see the location.

tip Another way to drop a pin is to tap the page curl to reveal the Maps settings and then tap the Drop Pin button.

To remove a pin, tap the  icon and then tap the Remove Pin button.

If you tap and hold the screen to drop a new pin, the previous one disappears. You can have only one purple pin on the map at one time.

Get Directions

I used to think that getting and printing directions from a mapping service on my computer was pretty cool, but now I don't even bother with the paper. It's easy to get directions between two locations in the Maps app—and not just driving directions, but walking and bus routes, too (where that information is available).

1. Tap the Directions button in the upper-left corner to switch to Directions mode. The Search field splits into two fields: the starting point and destination. The iPad assumes you want to start at your current location.

2. Enter a destination by performing a search in the second field (**Figure 8.10**).

Figure 8.10
Searching for a destination

To change the starting point, tap the first field and enter a search term or address. If you had previously dropped a pin, you can select its location by tapping the start field and selecting the address in purple text.

tip **If you're viewing information about an address, tap the Directions from Here or Directions To Here button to initiate a search.**

3. Tap Search on the onscreen keyboard to reveal the route, which appears as a blue line between the two points (**Figure 8.11**). For easier identification, the starting point is a green pin and the destination is a red pin.

Figure 8.11
Destination,
known

Route

4. Driving is the default mode of transport, but you don't need to be car-centric. Using the directions bar at the bottom of the screen, tap an icon to reveal bus route or walking directions.

The bus route is particularly helpful. Tap the clock icon on the directions bar to look up schedules and connections; you can also tap a bus stop to view the route number and departure time (**Figure 8.12**).

Follow the directions

As you travel, the Maps app can give you step-by-step directions (presumably so someone in the passenger seat can guide if you're driving; be safe out there, kids).

1. Tap the Start button in the directions bar.

Figure 8.12
Bus route information

2. Tap the arrow buttons to go to the next or previous step in the route. The bar lists directions for each step, and the route indicates where you are and where you've been (**Figure 8.13**). If you prefer a text list of directions, tap the button at the left of the bar.

Figure 8.13
A trip in progress

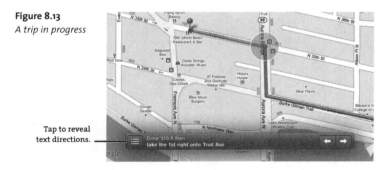

Tap to reveal text directions.

3. Continue tapping the arrow button until you've reached the destination.

tip When it's time to head home, tap the curved-arrow button between the search fields to swap the starting point and the destination.

Step-by-Step versus Turn-by-Turn

The directions in the Maps app doesn't advance automatically, the way some GPS devices do. Those offer turn-by-turn directions, where the device plots your course and tells you, audibly, when to make the next turn. The GPS chip inside the 3G iPad enables that same functionality using some third-party software. As of this writing, the only package available specifically for the iPad is CoPilot Live HD North America, but software for the iPhone is available and appears to work (although in the iPad's pixel-doubled emulation mode).

9

Organize Your Personal Information

The iPad isn't Apple's first foray into producing a PDA, or "personal digital assistant." The company created the category—and coined the term, even—with the Newton handheld. But the Newton wasn't adopted as broadly as its upstart competitor the PalmPilot, and when Steve Jobs returned to Apple in 1997, the Newton was killed. As Palm ascended and Windows Mobile devices appeared (and disappeared), people wondered when Apple would get back into the game. I think rumors of a new Apple PDA started floating around the day the Newton died.

A decade later, Apple finally created its modern PDA: the iPhone. Yes, it was a phone, but the phone aspect was just a way to put it into a familiar category. The iPhone, and now the iPad on a grander scale, is capable of storing and making accessible all of your personal information: your schedule, list of contacts, notes, snippets, ideas, and doodles.

Sync Personal Information

Although it's possible to create new events, contacts, and notes on the iPad (detailed in this chapter), most of that information probably already exists on your computer. There are two ways of transferring it to the iPad and keeping it updated: syncing through iTunes over the dock connector cable, or wirelessly using MobileMe or Microsoft Exchange.

iTunes sync

iTunes is the gateway between your data and the iPad, whether the data happens to be your music library or your schedule. With the iPad connected, do the following:

1. Select the iPad in the sidebar and click the Info tab (**Figure 9.1**). You'll find categories for contacts, calendars, "other" (notes and bookmarks), and mail accounts. (For details on mail accounts, see Chapter 4.)

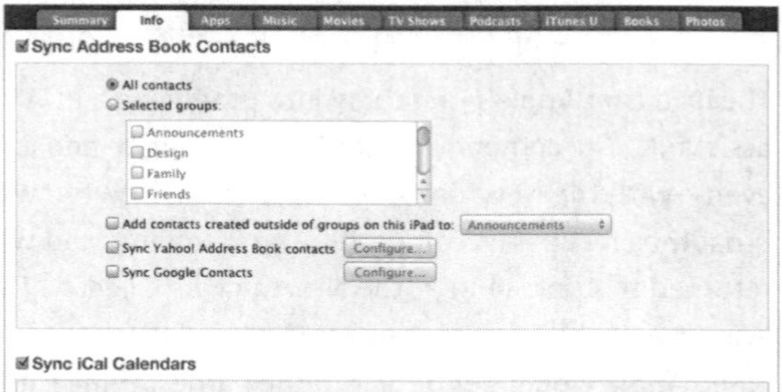

Figure 9.1
Syncing info in iTunes

2. Click the category checkboxes to enable syncing those items.

Under Mac OS X, contacts and calendars are synced with Address Book and iCal (or, more specifically, the underlying databases that those applications access). Under Windows, choose the data source from the pop-up menu in the category name; contacts, for example, can sync with Windows Contacts, Google Contacts, or Yahoo! Address Book by default.

3. Within each category, choose to sync all items or selected ones. For example, you may want to keep only business contacts and calendars on the iPad, in which case you'd acivate the Selected calendars option and then mark the checkboxes for specific calendars.

4. Click the Apply button to make the changes and sync the iPad. Future synchronizations will transfer updated information between the iPad and the computer.

MobileMe sync

As I mentioned in Chapter 1, the capability to synchronize personal information wirelessly is the main reason I subscribe to Apple's MobileMe service. If I change an event on my Mac, the change is propogated to my iPad, iPhone, and other computers within a minute or so. Syncing with MobileMe must be set up on the iPad, not in iTunes.

1. Go to Settings > Mail, Contacts, Calendars and tap the Add Account button.

2. Tap the MobileMe button.

3. Enter your name, MobileMe email address, and password. Tap Next.

4. Enable the services you want to sync (**Figure 9.2**, on the next page), and tap the Save button. After a few minutes, your MobileMe data transfers to the iPad.

tip While you're setting up MobileMe, be sure to activate the Find My iPad option. If your iPad is lost or stolen (or if you can't find it in your house), Find My iPad lets you view its location on a map in a Web browser, send a message or play a sound on the device, or remotely lock or wipe the memory. See Chapter 10 for more information.

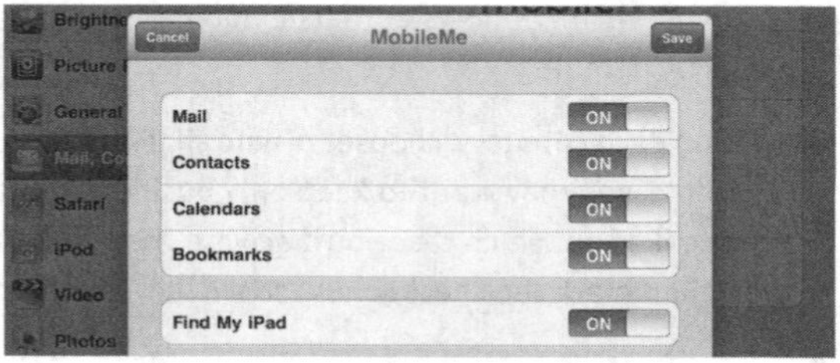

Figure 9.2
*Setting up
MobileMe
on the iPad*

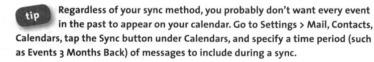

tip It's possible to sync via MobileMe and via iTunes. For example, you may want to sync your calendars via MobileMe but store only business contacts on the iPad. In that case you'd turn off the Contacts sync option for MobileMe and enable specific contact groups in the Info pane in iTunes.

tip Regardless of your sync method, you probably don't want every event in the past to appear on your calendar. Go to Settings > Mail, Contacts, Calendars, tap the Sync button under Calendars, and specify a time period (such as Events 3 Months Back) of messages to include during a sync.

Exchange sync

If your company manages its email, contacts, and calendars using Microsoft Exchange, you can tie the iPad into the system with little fuss.

1. Go to Settings > Mail, Contacts, Calendars and tap Add Account.

2. Tap the Microsoft Exchange button.

3. Enter your email address, username, and password (**Figure 9.3**). Tap Next.

4. After the information is verified, tap Next again.

5. Enable the services you want to sync (mail, contacts, and calendars) and tap the Save button. After a few minutes, the data transfers.

Figure 9.3
*Setting up
an Exchange
account*

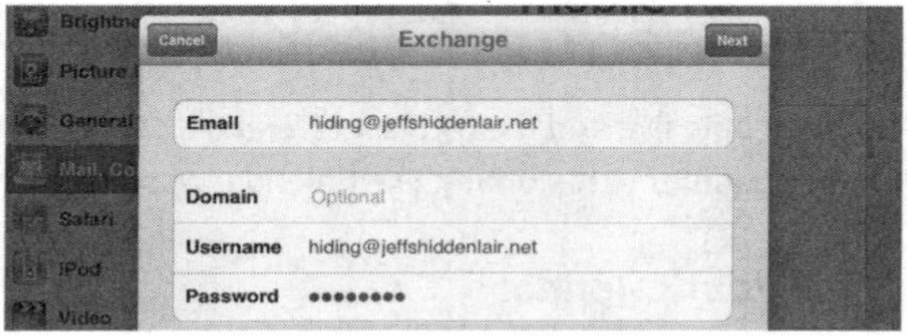

Cancel	Exchange	Next
Email	hiding@jeffshiddenlair.net	
Domain	Optional	
Username	hiding@jeffshiddenlair.net	
Password	••••••••	

note As of iPhone OS 3.2 (the first version of the iPad's software), you can sync contacts and events from only one Exchange account at a time. This limitation will be removed in iPhone OS 4 for iPad in Fall 2010.

Merge or Delete Contacts and Calendars

If you already have some contact or calendar information on the iPad when you add a MobileMe or Exchange account, you're asked if you want to merge the existing information with the new data **(Figure 9.4)**. Initially this dialog may be confusing, because it doesn't include a third option you may want: erase what's on the iPad and start over with the incoming records. However, it's coming. Tap the Do not Merge button, and in the next dialog that appears asking what you want to do with that existing information, tap Delete.

Figure 9.4
*Deleting
existing
contacts*

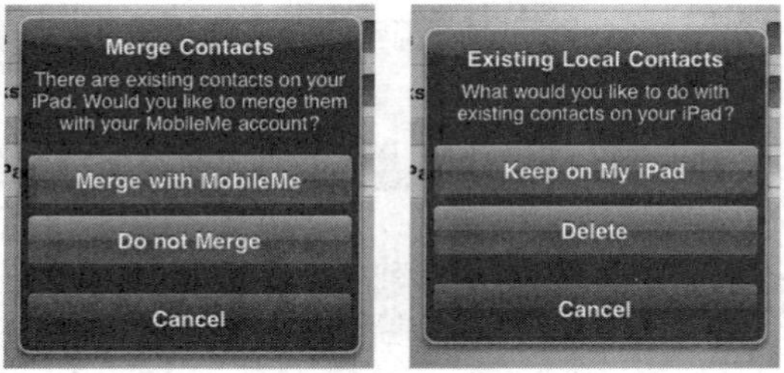

Merge Contacts
There are existing contacts on your iPad. Would you like to merge them with your MobileMe account?

Merge with MobileMe

Do not Merge

Cancel

Existing Local Contacts
What would you like to do with existing contacts on your iPad?

Keep on My iPad

Delete

Cancel

Manage Your Schedule

Some people live and die by their calendars, while others need to refer to their schedules occasionally. The Calendar app fits both personalities.

View your calendar

When you launch the Calendar app, your schedule appears in one of four views, all evoking the look of a paper-and-leather desk calendar. Tap a view button at the top of the screen.

Each view has its own focus—the Day view, for example, shows a schedule of the day on the right-hand page, with a small red pin indicating the current time. The day's events are listed at left (**Figure 9.5**).

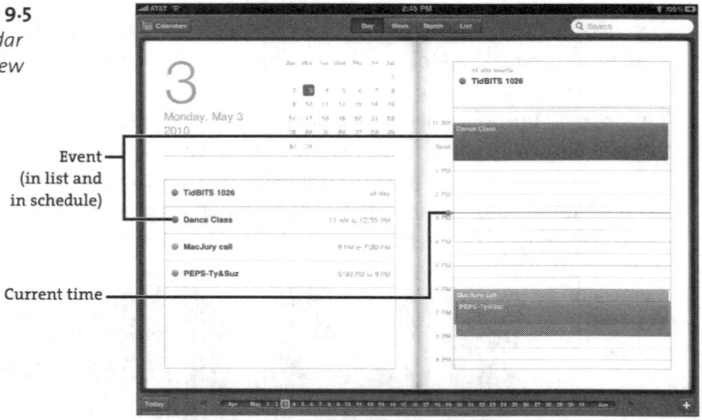

Figure 9.5
*Calendar
Day view*

Event —
(in list and
in schedule)

Current time —

Choose from a variety of ways to switch between dates:

- Tap the triangular buttons on either side of the timeline below the calendar to switch to the previous or next item, depending on the view. Tapping in the Week view, for instance, shifts to the next week.

- Tap a block of time on the timeline to jump directly to it (**Figure 9.6**).

Figure 9.6
Navigation bar

Previous button

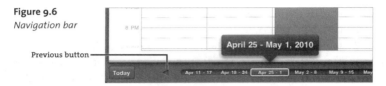

tip Touch and drag on the timeline to rapidly skim forward or backward in time. If you hold at the edge, the pop-up display indicates how far you're travling. Lift your finger to then display that date. This trick has some subtlety to it, too: After you've reached the edge, drag past it to make the dates fly by faster; drag your finger back to the edge to slow it down.

- Tap the Today button to jump to today's date in any view.

- Type a term into the Search box and tap the Search key on the onscreen keyboard. Touch any event to jump to it.

tip The Results popover that appears begins to find matches as you type, but I've found that it doesn't catch everything; you need to tap the Search key to perform a thorough search.

- In the Day view, tap a date in the calendar grid to jump to it.

- In the Month view, double-tap a date to switch to the Day view.

- When you're in the Week view and want to see a specific day in Day view, tap once on the date you want and then tap the Day button. If you just tap the Day button, you get that week's Monday entry.

note Despite appearing like a book of calendar pages, the Calendar app frustratingly does not respond to any common sense swipe gestures. So if you're swatting the screen trying to get to the next day, your technique isn't the problem: the app just doesn't support it.

Create or edit an event

A common scenario in my kitchen: while we're making dinner, my wife and I talk about what's happening during the week, specifically events our daughter attends. I often reach for the iPad to view the week, add new events, or edit current ones that have changed. I don't need to go upstairs to my computer to do that. And when I do get back to my desk, the changes are already applied, thanks to MobileMe syncing.

The following steps illustrate how to create a new event, but the steps are almost identical for editing existing events.

1. To create a new event, tap the + button in the lower-right corner. The Add Event popover appears.

   Editing an existing event initially depends on which view you're in:

   - In the Day view, tap it once.

   - To edit in the Week and Month views, tap an event once and then tap the Edit button that appears (**Figure 9.7**).

   - For the List view, tap an event to select it, then tap it again to bring up the editing popover.

Figure 9.7
Editing in Week view

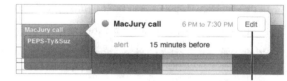

Click to edit

> **tip** The time for a new event is always based on the current time and date. However, if you first tap a day in the Week or Month views, the event initially is set on the date you tapped.

2. Type a name for the event in the Title field. You can also optionally add a location (**Figure 9.8**).

Figure 9.8
*Adding a title
and location*

3. Tap the Starts/Ends field and, using the dials below, set a starting date and time, and then an ending date and time (**Figure 9.9**). If the event doesn't have a specific time, enable the All-day option. Tap Done.

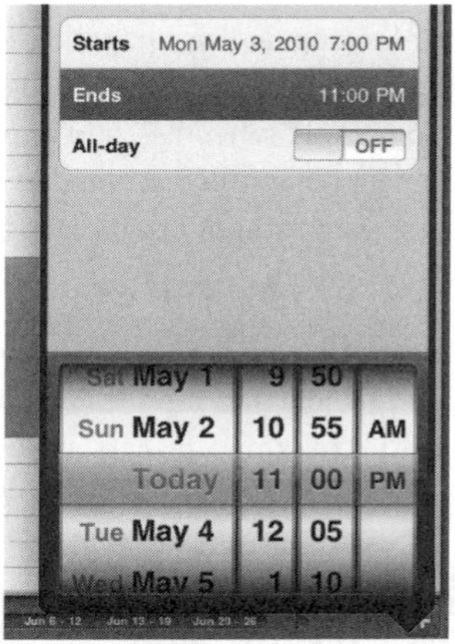

Figure 9.9
*The slot-machine
scheduler*

4. If the event is recurring, tap the Repeat button and specify how often: Every Day, Every Week, Every 2 Weeks, Every Month, or Every Year. Tap Done to return to the previous screen.

5. Tap the Alert button if you want an alarm to go off before the event, and then specify a time. Tap Done.

6. Choose which of your synced calendars the event will appear in. (You can specify a default calendar in Settings > Mail, Contacts, Calendars.)

tip The only time you can specify a calendar for a new event is when you first create the event. If you edit the entry later, the option to change calendars is not available.

7. Enter any miscellaneous details in the Notes field.

8. Tap Done to create or edit the event.

Hide or show calendars

The Calendar app tries hard to appear like a paper desk calendar, but here's one area where paper just wouldn't cut it. To juggle several kinds of events—business, personal, kids' schedules, and so on—you'd need separate physical calendars (or a handful of colored pens). Here you can include digital calendars for each category, color-code them, and show or hide them as you please.

New calendars must be created in your desktop software and synced to the iPad. Once there, in the Calendar app, tap the Calendars button and tap the ones you wish to hide (the checkmark disappears) (**Figure 9.10**). The events are still there, but they aren't cluttering up your calendar views.

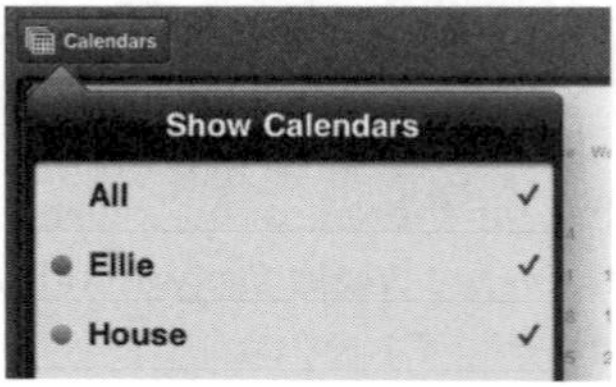

Figure 9.10
Choosing calendars to show

Manage Your Contacts

Over the years, my list of contacts has grown in size to the point where I know some of the information is out of date, but I don't have the time or desire to clean it all up. And really, I don't need to. The Contacts app stores it all for me so I can easily find a person's essential information.

Contacts also ties in to many other areas of the iPad, feeding email addresses for Mail and physical addresses for Maps. When you start typing someone's name in an outgoing email message, you're matching a record in the Contacts app—so you don't have to remember that your cousin Jeremy's address is actually b4conlov3r42lol@aol.com.

Find a contact

The Contacts app maintains the same spirit of the Calendar app, presenting your contacts in an address book (**Figure 9.11**). Flick through the list to browse for a contact, or use the tabs to advance through the alphabet.

Figure 9.11
The Contacts address book

Drag your finger down tabs to jump to contacts.

Tap a name to view its details.

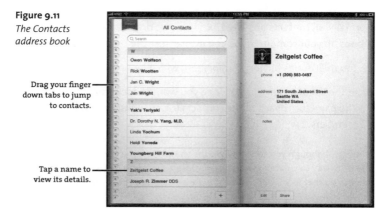

tip Contacts are listed in order of their last names, but you can change this preference. Go to Settings > Mail, Contacts, Calendars, tap Sort Order in the Contacts section, and change the option to "First, Last." The Display Order option in the same section dictates how each line appears (for example, changing that option to "Last, First" would make my name appear as Carlson Jeff). In either case, the last name appears in bold for easier identification.

If you know the name of the person or company you're trying to find (or even part of the name, or a detail that might be in their information) tap the Search field and begin typing. Results appear immediately, with the first one displayed at right (**Figure 9.12**).

Figure 9.12
Find a contact.

Normally, all contacts are listed, but if you've organized your contacts in groups on your computer, you can display just the contacts from a group.

1. Tap the Groups button at upper left, which looks like a red bookmark.

2. In the list of groups, tap the one you want to focus on (**Figure 9.13**). The page turns back to the contacts list, showing only that group's members.

note Although you can view groups on the iPad, the Contacts app offers no way to create new groups or move a person to a new group. You'll need to do that in your desktop software and then sync the changes to the iPad.

Figure 9.13
Selecting a group

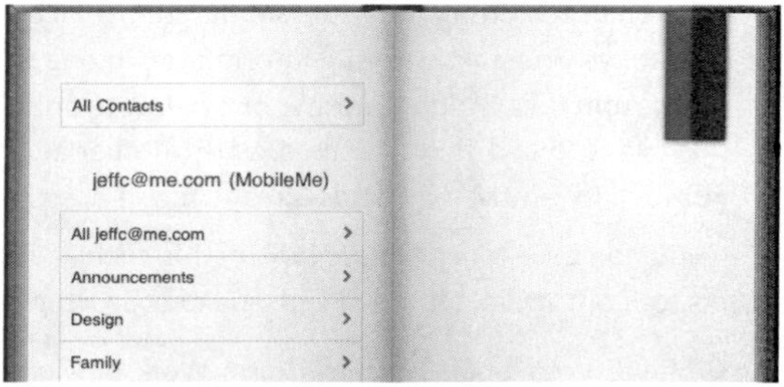

All Contacts	>
jeffc@me.com (MobileMe)	
All jeffc@me.com	>
Announcements	>
Design	>
Family	>

Create or edit a contact

I've learned the hard way that I possess a superhuman ability to repel important scraps of paper. Rather than jot down someone's contact information on the edge of an envelope, I prefer to add their details to the Contacts app so I know it won't get lost.

 Before you begin: If you want a new contact to belong to one of your groups, first make sure that group is the one selected.

1. Tap the New Contact button (+) to create a new record, or tap the Edit button to change details of an existing record.

2. Tap each relevant field and type the person's contact information (**Figure 9.14**).

Figure 9.14
Entering information for a new contact

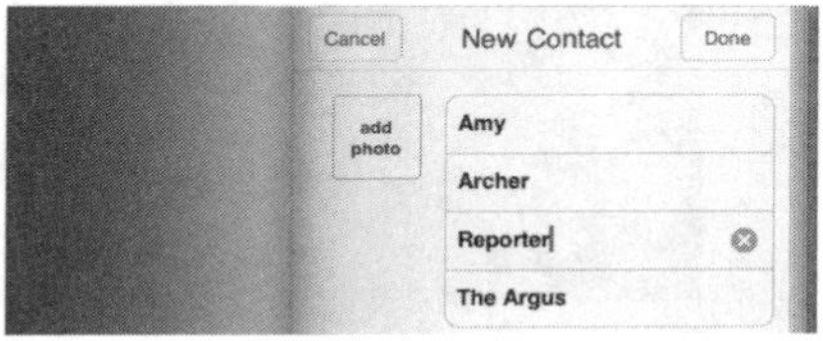

Cancel	New Contact	Done
add photo	Amy	
	Archer	
	Reporter	⊗
	The Argus	

3. A contact can contain multiple similar items, such as phone numbers. As soon as you start entering information in one field, the Contacts app automatically adds another one below it, anticipating that you may want to add, for instance, a work number and then a home number. To remove any fields already made, tap the red Delete button.

   If you don't see a field you're looking for, such as Job Title, scroll to the bottom of the list, tap Add Field, and choose from the options.

4. For fields with labels (such as Home, Work, or Mobile), tap the current label to view a popover containing alternates. If the one you want isn't listed, choose Add Custom Label and type your own.

5. To add a photo to the contact, tap the Add Photo box, which brings up your photo albums. Locate and tap an image to use, move and scale it to fit, and tap the Use button (**Figure 9.15**).

6. Tap Done when you're finished creating the contact. You can change details later by tapping the Edit button.

Figure 9.15
Grab an image from your Photos library.

tip If you haven't done so yet, be sure to create a record for yourself. Safari uses that information for its AutoFill feature (go to Settings > Safari > AutoFill, tap My Info, and specify your entry). It's also good for sharing your details with someone else.

Share a contact

Early handhelds from Palm included an infrared receiver that would let two Palm-wielding people "beam" contact information to each other. Not only was it incredibly geeky, it was extremely useful. In just a few seconds, one person's full contact information was in the other's contacts list. That was before devices were networked; now, we just bounce the same information out to the Internet and into someone's email inbox. To share a record from your Contacts list, do the following:

1. Locate the contact within the list and open it.

2. Tap the Share button. A new outgoing email address appears, containing a vCard file attachment that can be imported into most contact software.

3. Enter the email address of the person who will receive the contact.

4. Type a title in the Subject line (leaving the field blank could prevent or delay its delivery).

5. Tap the Send button.

Receive a shared contact

If you're on the receiving end of a shared contact, you can easily add someone's vCard to the Contacts list.

1. In the Mail app, locate the email message that includes the .vcf file attachment.

2. Tap the attachment to view the contact information (**Figure 9.16**, on the next page).

3. Tap either the Create New Content button or the Add to Existing Contact button to transfer the information to the Contacts app.

Figure 9.16
Adding a contact from email

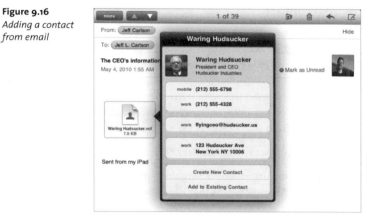

Delete a contact

If you find yourself standing in line somewhere with nothing to do, and suddenly feel the urge to purge old records from your Contacts list, do the following:

1. Tap a contact name to view it.

2. Tap the Edit button.

3. Scroll to the bottom of the information and tap the Delete Contact button.

4. In the confirmation dialog that appears, tap the Delete button. That contact is removed from the list.

Take Notes

Let's see, the iPad is roughly the size of a pad of paper, easy to hold in the hand, and capable of storing a lot of information. When you need to jot down some ideas, the Notes app is ready with a familiar yellow legal pad (mounted in a virtual leather holder, even, when viewed in landscape orientation).

Create a note

Here comes the hard part. Tap the New Note button (➕) and start typing. (Actually, not so hard.)

The first line of the note becomes the title, which appears in the toolbar and in the Notes list. In landscape orientation, that list sits off to the side (**Figure 9.17**); in portrait mode, tap the Notes button to bring up a popover containing all the notes you've stored.

Figure 9.17
The Notes app, viewed wide

Notes list —

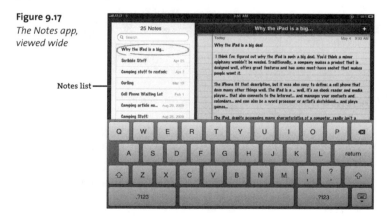

If you're looking for something in particular, enter a term in the Search field at the top of the Notes list (**Figure 9.18**).

Figure 9.18
*Searching notes,
viewed tall*

Search field

Edit notes

Tap a note in the list to view it. You can also tap the Previous and Next buttons at the bottom of the page to switch between notes (**Figure 9.19**).

Figure 9.19
*Notes controls,
with my own
homemade labels*

To edit, tap somewhere on the note to place the cursor, and start typing.

Delete a note

There are two ways to delete a note:

- With the note visible, tap the Trash button, then tap the Delete Note button.
- In the Notes list, swipe one finger across a note's title and tap the Delete button that appears.

Sync notes

We've already covered the mechanics of setting up the iPad to sync notes—it's a checkbox in the Info pane in iTunes. But where do the notes go on your computer? On the Mac, they show up in the Mail application. Under Windows, you need Microsoft Outlook 2003 or 2007.

Share notes

Tap the Mail icon at the bottom of the note to send its contents in an outgoing email message.

tip I'm a recent convert to a different note-taking app for the iPad: Simplenote (simple-note.appspot.com). It has a clean interface for writing notes, but its real strength is being able to sync its contents to the Web wirelessly. When you make changes, they're reflected at the Web site and on other devices you use that run Simplenote (such as the iPhone). I don't have to wait to sync over the dock connection cable to get the notes on my computer. For more bells and whistles, check out Evernote (www.evernote.com), a catch-all app and Web service that can store text, images, and audio for later.

Move Data Files To and From the iPad

The iPad envisions a future where people don't need to worry about file management. Using the Finder under Mac OS X or Windows Explorer on a PC leads to all sorts of gunk under the hood: *Where are my documents? If the desktop is right there behind my windows, why is it also a folder? Why can't I find the file I just saved?* We've coped with it for years because that was just the way it was. According to Apple's view of the world, an iPad owner shouldn't be exposed to all that. You create something. It's just there. End of story.

But we're not quite there yet. Like it or not, we still have to deal with files, and right now the process of getting them on and off the iPad is a bit of a mess.

There are currently three ways of transferring files that can be opened by applications on the iPad: send them via email, use iTunes as the gateway, or use a network service such as Apple's iWork.com, Dropbox, or SugarSync.

Email

Because the Mail app recognizes many common file types, you can send an email to yourself, receive the message on the iPad, and view the attachment. See Chapter 4 for more details.

Copy to Apps pane

Apps that can accept outside files appear at the bottom of the Apps pane in iTunes (**Figure 9.20**).

Figure 9.20
Sharing files in iTunes

Files on the iPad

1. Click the iPad app that you want to use to open your file.

2. Click the Add button and locate the file you want to transfer. Or, drag the file from the desktop to the Documents pane. The file is transferred immediately; you don't have to sync the iPad.

3. On the iPad, launch the app and use it to open the file (**Figure 9.21**).

Figure 9.21
Opening the file in Pages

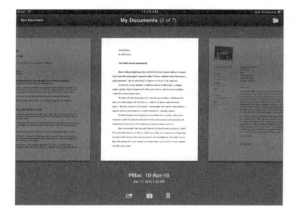

To get documents back out, reverse the process: connect to iTunes, and in the Apps pane, select an app, select the file you want, and either drag it to the desktop or click the Save To button and specify a destination.

tip Wait, you thought it would be that easy? Depending on the app, you may need to take an extra step. In Apple's iWork apps, you must export the file first to place it in a directory that is accessible to iTunes. Other apps may have a better option; be sure to check their documentation.

Sync with a network service

The other way to transfer files is via the Internet, using a service such as Apple's MobileMe or iWork.com, Dropbox (www.dropbox.com), or SugarSync (www.sugarsync.com). Files stored on the iPad are synchronized with a network server, which you can then access using your computer without needing to plug in a single cable.

Alas, that route is also still somewhat muddled, despite the obvious advantage it would present. To use the iWork apps as an example: You can send files to iWork.com, but it's not a direct process. First you must share the file to iWork.com, which sends the file via email instead of transferring it directly. To get the file onto your computer, you visit iWork.com, download the file, and *then* open it in an iWork app.

Dropbox and SugarSync sync the contents of folders on your computer and make them available on the iPad, where you can preview them or open them in supported apps (**Figure 9.22**). However, there's no way to edit a file and put it directly back onto the network service (although you can email it to a special SugarSync address to add it to your files).

I'm optimistic this whole process will be streamlined, but for now it's an elaborate kludge that works only if you're willing to jump through hoops.

Figure 9.22

Viewing a Word file in the Dropbox app

10

Be Secure

Most of the best qualities of the iPod can also be liabilities. It's portable, so you're more likely to take it with you to a coffee shop or to class where there's greater chance of losing it or having it stolen. Being out "in the wild" also increases the chance that the wireless network you connect to—or even someone at the next table—is scanning for sensitive data like credit card numbers. The iPad stores your personal digital information, so a thief would have access to your contact information.

Security isn't all cloak-and-dagger stuff, though. If you're sharing an iPad among your family, you may not want the kids to get online and download all of their favorite albums from the iTunes Store—on your credit card. With some reasonable precautions, you can make your iPad experience more secure.

Set a Passcode to Unlock

The easiest front-line measure you can take to improve the iPad's security is to set a four-digit passcode lock that must be entered when the iPad is woken from sleep.

1. Go to Settings > General and tap the Passcode Lock button.

2. Tap the Turn Passcode On button, which brings up the Set Passcode dialog (**Figure 10.1**).

Figure 10.1
Setting a passcode

3. Enter a four-digit code, then re-enter it to confirm.

4. The passcode dialog is initially set to appear whenever you wake the iPad. If that's too aggressive, tap the Require Passcode button and choose a timing during which the passcode isn't needed after entering it successfully once.

5. If you don't want anyone seeing your photos in the Picture Frame mode, turn the Picture Frame mode to Off. The Picture Frame button no longer appears on the lock screen.

6. To give the passcode lock some more teeth, enable the Erase Data
option (**Figure 10.2**). If an incorrect password is attempted 10 times,
the iPad wipes its memory.

Figure 10.2
*Erase Data
enabled*

General	Passcode Lock	
	Turn Passcode Off	
	Change Passcode	
Require Passcode		After 15 min. >
Picture Frame		ON
Erase Data		ON

Erase all data on this iPad after 10 failed passcode
attempts.

note After you set a passcode lock, you need to enter it whenever you want
to make changes to the passcode settings.

Use a VPN

When you connect to a public Wi-Fi hotspot, there's a real chance that
someone could be analyzing traffic on the network. The way to protect
against it (other than choose not to use public Wi-Fi networks, but that's
not a good option) is to set up a Virtual Private Network. A VPN estab-
lishes a secure connection to the Internet and protects your traffic from
prying eyes.

Your employer may have provided you with VPN connection information, or you might prefer to pay for a service such as PublicVPN (www.
publicvpn.com) or WiTopia (www.witopia.net). With the account information, configure the VPN settings so you can switch on the VPN when you
need it.

1. Go to Settings > General > Network, and tap the Add VPN Configuration button.

2. Enter the server and settings provided to you (**Figure 10.3**).

Figure 10.3
VPN settings

3. Tap the Save button.

When you want to activate the VPN, return to Settings > Network and tap the VPN On button. After the connection is made and authenticated, a VPN icon appears in the status bar (**Figure 10.4**).

Figure 10.4
VPN settings

VPN active

The VPN preferences screen keeps tabs on how long you've been connected; tapping the Status button also reveals more information such as the VPN server name and the IP address assigned to your iPad.

When you no longer need the connection, tap the VPN switch to Off.

Set Up Usage Restrictions

One unsurprising trend I've seen since the iPad was released is that it's a device that gets shared—whether you intend it to be shared or not. A good friend bought an iPad just before leaving on vacation, and he quickly discovered that it makes a great traveling companion. His young son used it on the plane to play educational games and watch videos, and then his wife used it to read ebooks in the evenings. He was happy to get his hands on the iPad late at night after everyone else went to bed.

The problem is that the iPad isn't set up like a Mac or PC, which have the capability to host multiple separate accounts. So, for example, my friend's email messages were exposed to anyone who wanted to go looking (or accidentally deleting), and he wasn't able to prevent the boy from stumbling onto Web sites that are inappropriate for a three-year-old.

That's where the iPad's Restrictions settings come in. They don't cover all possibilities—I'd like to see a future version of the operating system have a guest mode optimized for handing the iPad over to someone—but they do help prevent unwanted access.

1. Go to Settings > General > Restrictions to access the settings.

2. Tap the Enable Restrictions button.

3. Enter a Restrictions passcode in the keypad that appears, then enter it again for verification. This passcode is separate from the one you may have set up to lock the iPad.

4. In the first block of settings, determine which apps and services are allowed to run (**Figure 10.5**). When you switch an option to Off, the app disappears from the Home screen. When Location is disabled, the iPad doesnt' share its location with apps that request it.

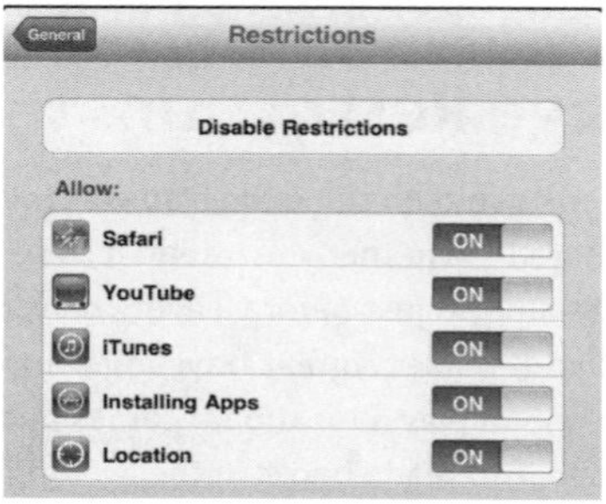

Figure 10.5
App restrictions

5. In the second block of settings, choose which media can be viewed (**Figure 10.6**). For example, you may wish to limit videos to movies rated no higher than PG when the kids are awake, and then change the rating or disable restrictions when you want to watch something rated R after the kids have gone to bed.

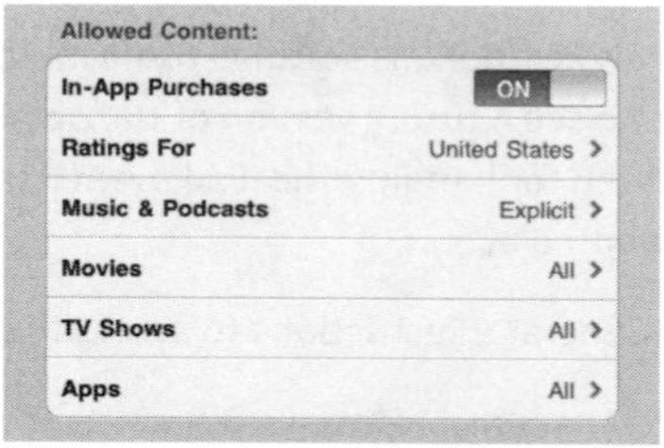

Figure 10.6
Media restrictions

Find My iPad

Apple's MobileMe has at least one feature that you may find is worth the yearly subscription fee, even if you don't touch any other part of the service. Find My iPad can locate your iPad on a map (even the Wi-Fi–only model, provided it's connected to a hotspot), send sounds or messages to it, or remotely erase its data if you think you'll never see it again.

Set Up Find My iPad

Do the following to make sure Find My iPad is active; you don't want to discover too late that you may not have set up the feature.

1. On the iPad, go to Settings > Mail, Contacts, Calendars and tap your MobileMe (me.com) account.

   (If you haven't created one yet, tap Add Account, tap MobileMe, and enter your account information.)

2. Set the Find My iPad option to On.

3. Tap Allow in the dialog that appears to grant the feature access to location data.

 For Find My iPad to work, the Location Services option (in the General pane) must be turned on.

Take Action on a Lost iPad

Whether your iPad has fallen behind the back cushion on the couch or fallen into the wrong hands, you can take several actions using Find My iPad to help locate it.

- **Find:** In a Web browser, go to www.me.com and sign in. Then click the Find My iPad icon. After a few minutes, your iPad should appear with a map noting its location (**Figure 10.7**).

  Unless there's a solid fix on the iPad's signal, the location may not be too accurate. After a few minutes, a better location is resolved. You can also click the Update Location button to refresh the view, which is if the iPad seems to be on the move.

Figure 10.7

Find My iPad, found

Find My iPad icon —

iPad location —

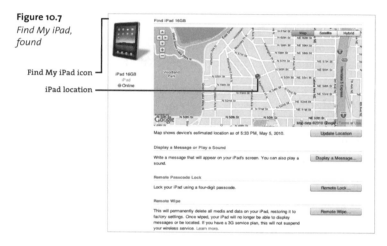

- **Display a Message:** If you suspect you've simply misplaced the iPad in your home (where the top-down map wouldn't provide enough resolution), click the Display a Message button. Enter a message and optionally mark the option to Play a sound for 2 minutes with this message (**Figure 10.8**). (The sound resembles a submarine's sonar ping and plays loud, despite the iPad's volume setting.)

Figure 10.8
Find My iPad message being sent and received

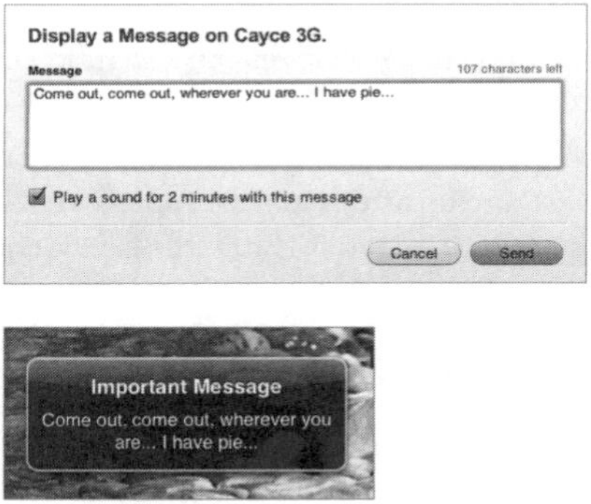

tip   I was trying to be cute in the figure above, but if you think someone might have picked up the iPad, you could use the message feature to alert that the iPad is lost, offer a reward for its return, or just include a contact email or phone number.

- **Remote Lock:** This feature locks the iPad immediately (even if someone is in the middle of using the device) with a four-digit passcode of your choosing. Pick a code that's different from the screen unlock code in case whoever has the iPad might know your code. The new passcode replaces the one you set in the Passcode Lock settings on the iPad.

- **Remote Wipe:** If you think the iPad is gone for good, or you don't want to risk that someone may get past the passcode and access sensitive information, click the Remote Wipe button. You're asked to confirm your choice and then click the Erase All Data button (**Figure 10.9**).

Figure 10.9
Are you sure?

All data on the iPad is automatically hardware-encrypted, so performing a remote wipe actually changes the encryption key; it doesn't remove any data (but the data that's left is useless). As a result, wiping is fast, taking only a minute and a half.

If the iPad does turn up after a remote wipe, connect it to your computer and restore everything from the last backup.

Encrypt iPad Backup

Speaking of the iPad's backup, you can perform remote wipes all day and it won't matter if the computer you sync with was stolen along with the iPad. You can get some measure of relief if you also encrypt the iPad data backup that's stored on the computer's hard disk.

In iTunes with the iPad selected in the sidebar, go to the Summary pane and enable the Encrypt iPad backup option (**Figure 10.10**).

Figure 10.10
Encrypt iPad backup option

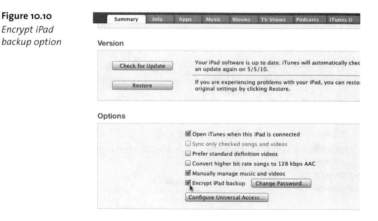

Troubleshooting

A comment I've heard frequently, especially among jaded tech writers who deal with new hardware all the time, is that the iPad doesn't feel like a "1.0" release. When something truly new comes out, not just an update to something familiar, we expect to run into problems that the engineers could not have anticipated under lab conditions.

And yet, the iPad is surprisingly stable. Since receiving mine on the first day they were available in the U.S., I've experienced a handful of application crashes and only one hard freeze that made the iPad unresponsive— all easily fixed.

But that's the point, isn't it? It should all just work, and for most of the iPad experience, it does. When it doesn't, a few simple steps will solve the majority of problems that crop up.

Restart the iPad

I don't want to sound flip, but restarting the iPad is almost a universal cure-all. If the iPad's internal working memory gets full or fragmented, you may see problems or sluggish performance.

1. Press and hold the Sleep/Wake button on the case. A red slider labeled Slide to power off appears at the top of the screen.

2. Drag the slider. After a few seconds, the iPad turns off.

3. Count to ten, and then press the Sleep/Wake button to restart the iPad.

When an App Crashes

The iPhone OS, which runs the show, is designed so that if an app crashes, it does it without affecting other processes. A crashed app typically just disappears, at which point you'll find yourself back at the Home screen. Tap the app to launch it again and you should be fine.

If the problem persists, check for an update at the App Store. Also read the release notes for the app; developers must submit their apps to Apple for approval, and if a bug has crept in, there's a lag between when an updated version is submitted and when it becomes available.

If that doesn't work, delete the app from the iPad and reinstall it.

Reinstall an App

If the copy of an app on the iPad has become corrupted for some reason, try a fresh copy.

1. On the iPad, touch and hold the app's icon until all of the icons begin to shake, then tap the Delete button (the X) to remove the app.

2. Connect the iPad to your computer and perform a sync.

3. In the Apps pane within iTunes, locate the app and make sure it's enabled for syncing. When you delete an app from the iPad, you still have a backup version in iTunes.

4. Click the Apply button to re-sync and transfer the app back to the iPad.

If that doesn't solve the crashing problem, and it seems clear that other people are not having the same issue, try starting over with the app.

1. Delete the app from the iPad.

2. Also delete the app from iTunes: Click the Apps icon in the sidebar, locate the app in the list, and press Delete. Verify that you want to remove the app (**Figure 11.1**), and in the next dialog choose to move the file to the Trash.

Figure 11.1
Deleting an app from iTunes

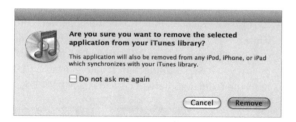

Are you sure you want to remove the selected application from your iTunes library?

This application will also be removed from any iPod, iPhone, or iPad which synchronizes with your iTunes library.

☐ Do not ask me again

Cancel   Remove

tip To find an app in iTunes easily, switch to the list view and then click the Kind column heading. Apps are then grouped by device, such as "iPad app" and "iPhone/iPod touch/iPad app".

3. Go to the App Store (either within iTunes or on the iPad) and purchase the app again. Since you'd bought it previously, you aren't charged again (**Figure 11.2**).

Figure 11.2
Downloading an app again

You have already purchased this item. To download it again for free, select OK.

Cancel   OK

4. Sync the iPad if you downloaded the app from iTunes. If you downloaded it on the iPad, launch the app.

Connectivity Issues

The iPad was designed to connect to the Internet over a wireless connection, so not having that connection can be frustrating. If you can't connect, try the following:

- Look for a connection indicator in the upper-left corner of the screen (**Figure 11.3**). The Wi-Fi icon appears when you're connected to a Wi-Fi network. If you're using a Wi-Fi–only iPad, the lack of the Wi-Fi icon means you have no connection. If you're using a 3G iPad, as shown here, the cellular 3G network is active when Wi-Fi isn't available.

Figure 11.3
Wireless connection icons

Wi-Fi   3G cellular

note Many iPad owners have reported Wi-Fi flakiness with the first round of iPads that came out in April 2010, such as dropping the network unexpectedly, or getting poor reception in areas where other devices connect well. My colleague Glenn Fleishman wrote about the problem in TidBITS (see "Some iPad Uses Suffer Wi-Fi Woes," db.tidbits.com/article/11166). I'm optimistic that the problem will be fixed in a software update.

- On a 3G iPad, the network indicator icon and signal strength bars appear even if you haven't paid for an active data plan. If the signal is there but you can't get online, make sure you've activated a data plan, or that you're not at the end of the 250 MB limit for the $14.99 plan (see Chapter 1 for more information).

- Try turning off Wi-Fi and turning it back on again. In Settings > Wi-Fi, set the Wi-Fi switch to Off, wait a minute, and then set it back to On.

- Similarly, try turning off the cellular radio on a 3G iPad and then turning it back on. In Settings > Cellular Data, toggle the Cellular Data switch.

- In the Wi-Fi settings, tap the Detail (⊙) button next to the name of the active network to view its advanced settings (**Figure 11.4**). Then, tap the Renew Lease button, which makes the iPad request a new temporary IP address from the Wi-Fi base station.

Figure 11.4
Renewing the Wi-Fi network lease

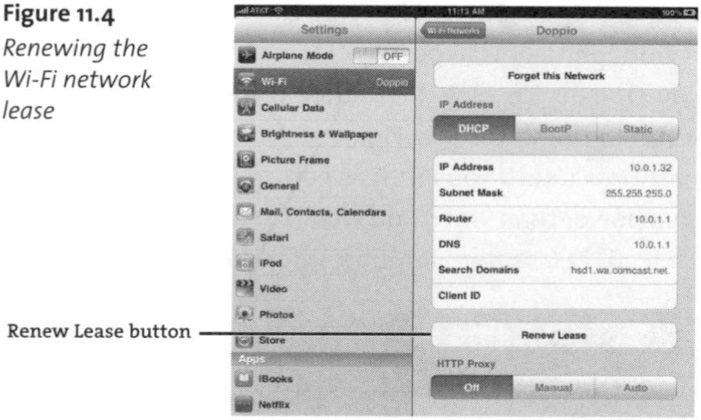

Renew Lease button

If the iPad Doesn't Appear in iTunes

The iPad needs to connect to iTunes, but sometimes that may not happen. Try these solutions, in order of least to most inconvenient:

- Make sure iTunes is up to date. On the Mac, go to the iTunes menu and choose Check for Updates. Under Windows, choose Check for Updates under the Help menu.

- Connect the iPad to a different USB port on your computer.

- Use a different sync cable.

- Restart the iPad and the computer.

- Download a new copy of iTunes (from www.apple.com/itunes/) and reinstall the software on the computer.

- If none of those suggestions work under Mac OS X, you may need to replace the Apple Mobile Device Service. Find detailed instructions at the following article: support.apple.com/kb/HT1747.

Battery Issues

The iPad's battery requires more power to charge than what many computers put out through their USB ports, which can be a shock to some people who buy the device, plug it into their computers, and see a Not Charging indicator in the status bar (**Figure 11.5**). Actually, the iPad *is* charging, but at a very low rate. If you left it asleep and connected overnight, you'd see more power than when you went to sleep. See the sidebar "Recharging the iPad" in Chapter 1 for more information.

Figure 11.5
*Not Charging
indicator*

If battery life seems dramatically worse than it did when you bought the iPad, contact Apple about possibly getting a replacement under warranty.

If you're out of warranty and the iPad "requires service due to the battery's diminished ability to hold an electrical charge," in Apple's words, then you can take advantage of Apple's battery replacement service. For $99, Apple will replace the entire iPad (so be sure you've synchronized it before sending it off). See www.apple.com/support/ipad/service/battery/ for more information.

Reset the iPad

If the iPad does not respond to input at all, it needs to be reset.

Press and hold the Sleep/Wake and Home buttons simultaneously for 10 seconds, or until the Apple logo appears. Resetting does not erase the iPad's memory.

Restore the iPad to Factory Defaults

If you continue to have problems, or if you simply want to start over from scratch, you can restore the iPad to its initial state. Remember, this action erases your data from the iPad, so make sure you sync first (if the iPad is working properly) to back up your data.

1. Connect the iPad to your computer.

2. In iTunes, select the iPad in the sidebar and click the Restore button in the Summary pane.

3. In the confirmation dialog that appears, click the Restore button (**Figure 11.6**, on the next page).

Figure 11.6

Restoring the iPad to its initial state

The first time you do this, iTunes downloads a clean version of the iPad's software; subsequent restores pull the data from your hard disk. In either case, you must have an active Internet connection, because iTunes verifies the iPad with Apple's servers.

4. Wait. iTunes copies the data to the iPad, which installs it. After a few minutes, the iPad is ready.

5. In iTunes, choose a backup to restore to the device. Or, you can opt to set it up as a new iPad with just the data that ships on it.

tip For more detailed options, see the following article at Apple's Web site: "Update and restore alert messages on iPhone, iPad, and iPod touch" (http://support.apple.com/kb/TS1275).

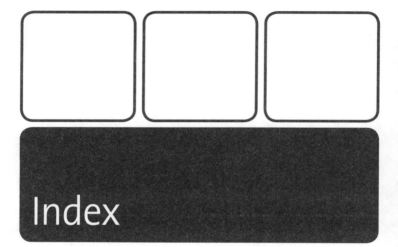

Index

Meet Creative Edge.

A new resource of unlimited books, videos and tutorials for creatives from the world's leading experts.

Creative Edge is your one stop for inspiration, answers to technical questions and ways to stay at the top of your game so you can focus on what you do best—being creative.

All for only $24.99 per month for access—any day any time you need it.

creative
edge

creativeedge.com